THE LIFE AND VIOLENT TIMES OF
HAL C. BANKS

Waterfront Warlord

Peter Edwards

KEY PORTER BOOKS

Canadian Cataloguing in Publication Data

Edwards, Peter, 1956–
Waterfront warlord

Includes index.
ISBN 1-55013-013-7

1. Banks, Hal, 1909– . 2. Seafarers' International Union of Canada—Biography. 3. Trade-unions—Canada—Officials and employees—Biography. 4. Crime and criminals—Canada—Biography. I. Title.

HD6525.B35E39 1987 331.88'1162388'0924 C87-093335-3

Key Porter Books Limited
70 The Esplanade
Toronto, Ontario
Canada, M5E 1R2

Design: Don Fernley
Typesetting: Compeer Typographic Services Limited
Printing and binding: Gagné Printing

Photo Credits:

CanaPress, 88 (top); CP/*Gazette*, 88 (bottom); 89, 90; CP/Canada-Wide, 91; 92, 93, 95, 97; CP/Canada-Wide, 98; 99, 100
Peter Edwards, 87, 101, 102
La Presse, 96
Toronto Star, 94

Printed and bound in Canada

87 88 89 90 6 5 4 3 2 1

For Lori,
Sarah and James.
All my love
always.

Banks is capable, decisive, egocentric, intolerant and ruthless. He is the stuff of the Capones and the Hoffas of whom the dictators throughout history, from the earliest times to the totalitarians, Hitler and Stalin, are prototypes. He is a bully, cruel, dishonest, greedy, powerhungry, contemptuous of the law. In his mouth, the use of the word ''democracy'' is sheer blasphemy. For him the ''big lie'' and the failure to remember are ever-ready weapons and shields.

Justice T.G. Norris, Industrial Inquiry Commission on the Disruption of Shipping

Banks had been of real service to Canada in the labour troubles of some years ago on the Great Lakes.

Censored Cabinet document, dated June 30, 1954, stamped ''Top Secret''

I've had to fight finks and scabs and look out for my boys. It's a tough position and sometimes I haven't had time to be a gentleman. But I've done my job.

Hal Chamberlain Banks

AUTHOR'S NOTE

I was working at the *Toronto Sun* in September 1985 when, an hour before deadline, the news came that Hal Banks had died in a San Francisco hospital. Assistant city editor Sean McCann scrambled to get a suitable obituary written before we went to press. It was simply too big a story to let slide by. More than twenty years after his flight from Canada, there was still mystery and electricity attached to Banks' name.

That week I did a title search of Canadian and American books, and was startled to see that there was nothing about Banks. So I decided to write one myself, drawing from as many personal interviews as I could get. Also, with the aid of Access to Information and Freedom of Information requests as well as searches of private papers in archives, I would try to shed some light on the rumours that still lingered about Banks' blackmail and coercion of top Ottawa and Washington figures. The fruit of that research is this book.

I couldn't help but wonder if much of the excitement surrounding Banks was simply media hype from the Toronto *Telegram—Toronto Star* newspaper circulation wars of the 1960s. On the other hand, I thought, perhaps it was the product of some Canadian insecurity that made us want a villain who could compare with the worst the U.S. could offer. But after more than a year's study, I found that Banks was even more bizarre and complex than his journalistic portraits suggested. He was, by his very nature, sensational. In fact, of the millionaires, communists, former cabinet ministers, thugs (including a CIA-agent-turned-gunrunner for Muammar al-Qaddafi) and Banks family members I interviewed, virtually all admitted that they had never met anyone else remotely like him. The one exception was a former employee who likened Banks' charisma to that of Mussolini.

Obtaining interviews about Banks was not always easy. His name, even now, has lost little of its power to intimidate. One beating victim was still afraid of him, more than twenty years after being attacked and a year after Banks' death. Another man I approached, a ship's captain, feared that the political implications of what he might reveal would hurt Canada's chances of developing its merchant marine. And there were many people who, having either backed or actively worked for Banks, had gone on to respectable and lucrative careers. Understandably, they were not eager to be connected with Banks. Two of Banks' former union officers agreed to turn over information if the financial incentive was high enough. (The offers were refused.) Other respondents preferred the violent approach: one former Banks lieutenant warned that he would string parts of my anatomy from his necktie, should his name appear in the book. Finally, there were cases where I was simply ignored, such as the time I requested permission to study the files of the Seafarers' International Union at its Maryland offices.

Offsetting the impediments to my research, however, were an equal number of people who gave generously of their time in helping me: Stephen Schwartz, author and historian of the Sailors' Union of the Pacific, an invaluable source of information, as well as a delight to work with, and whose influence can be found throughout this work; John Droeger, who was also extremely helpful, and great company; in addition, I would like to thank Mrs. Jean Crowe, who allowed me access to her late husband Harry's papers. Much of my work consisted of following up on Harry Crowe's original suspicions, and I stand in profound admiration of his courage, intelligence and commitment.

The late Bill Dodge of the Canadian Labour Congress was extremely co-operative in providing me with both a lengthy interview and valuable information from his personal files. Although suffering considerable pain from the cancer that killed him less than two months after the interview, Dodge was determined that the story of Hal Banks be accurately documented, and gave me access to a recorded interview that he had conducted on the subject with the late Bill Smith of the CBRT. Henry Rhodes of the CLC was also helpful and gave me material from his personal files as well, as did Harry Mockeridge.

Captain David Walsh, who has every reason to be proud of his father's conduct, was helpful and pleasant, as were his parents. My thanks to journalists Douglas Fisher, Peter Maas and Wilfrid List, who allowed me access to their personal papers, as well as providing personal interviews; also to Robert Reguly (the man who found Banks when two governments said he couldn't be found) who was unselfish with his knowledge and time.

Also deserving of thanks are Andy MacFarlane and John Sawatsky for their aid in pursuing grants; *Toronto Sun* librarian Julie Kursh, who gave me access to the *Sun*'s clipping files on Banks; editor Rick Orchard of the *Toronto Star* for all his help; Dawn Dobson of the CLC for her patience and generosity; Jim Whelan and Peter Delottinville, who helped educate me in the mysteries of the National Archives; N.N. Dainard of the Metro Toronto Library newspaper department; L.J. Keller of the Library of Congress in Washington; author William Kaplan; R.J. Gingerich of the CBRT; Dr. Eileen Herridge; banker Blanche Quinn; J. and S. Edwards; L. and S. Cox and writer Scott Young.

Research for the book involved numerous trips to Ottawa and Montreal, as well as two trips to San Francisco and Brooklyn and side trips to smaller centres. My research documents filled five filing cabinet drawers, and my collection of taped interviews is substantial. Papers and tapes will be turned over to an archive for the benefit of anyone doing further study on Banks. On-the-record interviews are listed in the back of the book. There were also about twenty-five off-the-record interviews, which included beating victims, former cohorts of Banks and former union office-workers. Conversations reported in this book are taken either from previous testimony of participants or from my interviews. The same applies to passages which give emotional responses of subjects. No comments were fabricated or embellished by the author.

Among the materials opened expressly for this project were more than a dozen boxes of previously closed Norris Commission records. There were also previously sealed documents from the Department of Citizenship and Immigration, the RCMP and the FBI. Unfortunately, Freedom of Information legislation notwithstanding, it appears that more government files on Banks are closed than open, even after Banks' death.

An Ontario Arts Council grant of $1,000 aided in the preparation of this work.

Finally, and most of all, I would like to thank my wife Lori for her encouragement, thoughtful editing and love. She accomplished the impossible, sharing an apartment for more than a year with me—and the spirit of Hal C. Banks.

1

All publicity is good—even the bad stuff.

Hal C. Banks

Hal Banks had no unifying philosophy of life, but rather an overpowering basic urge: to seize power and maintain it. He was drawn to power like a shark is drawn to blood and, like a shark, Banks only moved forward.

Banks was just another California waterfront thug when he was brought to Canada in early 1949 by a combination of government, shipping and right-wing union interests. His six-month assignment was to crush the supposedly Moscow-led Canadian Seamen's Union, and he did it with unparalleled speed and ruthlessness. But when his job was done, it was clear that Hal C. Banks had no intention of heading back to the San Francisco Bay area to resume his position as an underling in the Seafarers' International Union.

Instead, he built what he bragged was the most expensive union hall in Canada. His new office wasn't on the windy streets of the Montreal dockside, but in the St. James Street financial district, where the real power lay. And to Banks, power meant control. So anyone visiting his expansive, third-floor executive suite had to pass first through a gauntlet of numerous locked doors, as well as the menacing scrutiny of union strongarms such as 250-pound Bob Aitken or 270-pound Eldon Richardson. Occasionally, visitors would be kept waiting more than an hour for the sheer sport of it. Then, as at least one millionaire shipper discovered, you might not be allowed to sit down.

But even those permitted to sit weren't spared Banks' intimidation tactics. His desk and swivel chair were mounted high on a concrete dais, exaggerating both the size of the already-imposing Banks and the insignificance of his guests. (Banks got the idea from a popular book on power psychology, one of the rare times anyone can remember him reading.) The effect was further enhanced by adding extra padding to his swivel chair, then cranking it up as high as it would go. Conversely, the legs of the guest chairs were considerably shorter than normal. Later he would install a dome in a false ceiling above his desk which made his gravelly baritone sound even more menacing.

At his fingertips was a battery of telephones, providing instant contact with port agents across Canada and phone-equipped union cars in Montreal. Beside the phone was a well-polished brass console with an array of buttons that controlled, among other things, Banks' intercom system. With it, Banks boasted, he could monitor activities in any room in the building, ''except the women's washroom.'' (At least one colleague has remarked, however, that this is probably the first place Banks would have had a microphone installed.) Other buttons allowed him to lock the doors en route to his office and stop his private elevator between floors. Typically, a guest who had angered Banks might find himself sharing an elevator with the likes of union enforcers Aitken or Richardson. By the time the elevator reached street level, the visitor would have been reminded—painfully—that he hadn't been smart. Banks could also program the elevator so that, if he wished to be left alone, it would not stop at his penthouse, thereby affording him the twentieth-century equivalent of a medieval moat.

The buttons at Banks' fingertips also allowed him to control the suite's lighting, open and close the curtains and operate his wall-mounted, remote-controlled television—a rarity in the early 1950s—complete with retractable cover. Nearby, set into the wall of Banks' office was his four-foot-long, oak-trimmed goldfish tank. One might imagine that Banks kept the fish because they reminded him of the sea; perhaps more importantly, however, they made no demands and were totally at his mercy. As with his men, he could watch their every move.

Journalist Syd Katz, who profiled Banks in 1955 for *Maclean's* magazine, understood the feeling of being watched. At the beginning of the interview, Banks looked down from his dais and said, "I knew you were writing a story about me as soon as you did yourself." Then he listed the people Katz had interviewed for the article and the questions he had asked them. By way of explanation he added, "I've got ways of getting information."

Banks recognized that the perception of being powerful was an important part of power itself. As he explained to Katz: "I'm no first trip mess boy. All publicity is good—even the bad stuff. My name's in the papers any number of times. The membership laps it up. They figure I'm a going concern. I don't need a publicity agent. People are always writing and talking about me anyway."

In fact, Banks did hire a public relations firm, whose ranks included a former *Montreal Star* reporter. The official function of the PR men was to type out press releases and publish the union newspaper, *Canadian Sailor*. But other duties might include supplying hookers for a Banks party or bribing a hotel switchboard operator to provide access to private telephone conversations. The press, Banks believed, could be controlled if the appropriate incentives were offered.

To a certain extent, Banks was right. Stories were rife that he had members of the Montreal media in his back pocket, and a check of Montreal *Gazette*, *Star* and *Herald* files from the early 1950s shows surprisingly little negative press about him. As former Toronto *Telegram* reporter Frank Drea recalls: "You crossed over the Ottawa River and the guy was one of the saints of our time. He was paying for it by the inch." Drea was once offered an envelope full of bills while chatting with one of Banks' Seafarers' International Union officials at the St. Charles tavern in Toronto, back when the St. Charles catered to a largely heterosexual clientele. Drea angrily refused the offer.

Money was only one of Banks' incentives, however, as *Maclean's* reporter Katz discovered when he shared a drink with Banks in a downtown Montreal bar. Seemingly on cue, they were joined by comely, aggressive young women, and Katz sensed he had been set up for more than conversation. Katz had heard the rumours about Banks' Drummond Street luxury apartment, with its mirrored walls and full stock of liquor, all paid for with union funds. On the other side of the two-way mirrors, the stories went, were SIU men with cameras recording the sexual activities of shippers, unionists, MPs and even Cabinet ministers consorting with hookers. Katz gulped down his drink and quickly left the bar, telling Banks he had to run to an appointment.

Banks learned to adopt a chummy attitude with members of the press, whom he privately called ''typewriter prostitutes.'' They were useful for sending out thinly veiled warnings to the rank-and-file that he was not a man to be crossed. On one occasion, reporter Frank Drea was in the middle of a friendly chat with Banks when a news photographer approached them. Banks' expression suddenly hardened for the benefit of the camera and he bit his cigarette between his incisors in a snarling pose. Eddie Roworth, formerly a reporter-photographer with the *Toronto Star*, also remembers that SIU thugs planning violence on the picket lines would often wait until newspaper photographers arrived to record the action. Yet, even when confronted by reports of having instigated the violence, Banks demonstrated a certain rollicking charm as he denied accusations of wrongdoing. Reporters who looked directly into his pale blue eyes, however, were often left with a chilling feeling. As Peter C. Newman, then a young reporter for *The Financial Post*, commented, Banks had eyes that ''rest on you with a glance straight as a rifle barrel.''

Banks was a man of contradictions, and his appearance showed it. Although he owned dozens of shoes and scores of suits—most handmade from Montreal's noted Tony the Tailor shop—he made no effort to conceal the marks of a less elegant past. He was missing the tips of his left thumb and middle finger and had purplish scars across his hand. He told the press that they were souvenirs from a knife fight with a drug-crazed Filipino sailor. Others would hear how he had slashed his hand grabbing a knife out of the hand of an attacker on a west coast tanker. The story went that he then pummelled his enemy and stuffed him into the hold of a ship.

Banks had a permanent lump on his forehead from a Pacific coast union skirmish and claimed to have a bullet scar on his hip from being caught in a crossfire in Montreal in 1949 during the war with the Canadian Seamen's Union. His skin had the look of oily leather and his gruff voice matched his overall appearance. No matter how expensive the suit over his ursine figure, there was never a chance that Banks would be mistaken for the statesman he so desperately longed to be. And while he often feigned refinement and education in the presence of those business, union and government leaders he sought to control, Hal Banks was very much a product of the San Francisco waterfront he had left behind.

2

He never talked about his past, period.

Banks' old San Francisco waterfront associate,
Ed Turner, longtime SIU official

There's a hill in Richmond, California, that young Hal Banks would have known as Nichol's Knob. Climb it and you see the San Francisco Bay area at its most beautiful—and most desolate.

Across the bay lies Marin County, where you can find some of the most expensive real estate in the United States, a land of eucalyptus groves and luxury living. Turning slightly, you can see the urban sophistication of San Francisco in the distance. Just in front of it lies the rocky island of Alcatraz, former home of America's most notorious criminals, including Machine Gun Kelly and Al Capone. Another turn and your view is interrupted by an even more startling incongruity, the unreal and enormous Chevron refinery, operated by Standard Oil a half-century ago. Fresh and natural breezes are often soured by a sudden gust of nauseating refinery effluents. Not surprisingly, better homes in Richmond are found on the far side of Nichol's Knob, away from the stench of the refinery.

Sit on Nichol's Knob at night and your eyes aren't drawn up to the heavens, but rather down to the refinery's endless and otherworldly field of flickering lights. The sight says something about the soul of Hal Banks: a vision of awesome power, of satanic beauty; a place where men are dwarfed by the giant manifestation of technology and engineering. Given such an environment, one can imagine that a sailor, like the young Hal Banks, could easily be swallowed up in its dizzying, dehumanizing power.

Standard Oil was attracted to the Richmond side of the Bay

because it was undeveloped, and its labour had yet to become organized by the unions of the San Francisco side. Companies didn't just operate in Richmond, they ran it. Respectable authorities and not-so-respectable strongarms made sure things were kept that way.

A sailor like Banks would pass through the company gates, board a company boat carrying just his duffel bag, then sail past the flickering, artificial lights to a tanker resting offshore. The trip was as much psychological as physical: from that point onward, Standard Oil would control his life twenty-four hours a day for months at a time. Being subject to such absolute power could make a man feel very small or very hostile, or both.

The tankers of Standard Oil were manned by the lowest caste of the west-coast sailing order. Since losing a violent strike in 1934, these sailors were totally at the company's mercy, and other sailors couldn't help but regard them with some degree of contempt. As men without enough self-respect to demand their rights, they couldn't be classified as scabs in the technical sense of the word. But they certainly weren't part of the union fraternity.

Hal Banks came to work the tankers of Richmond along a route he later tried to hide with grandiose lies and hostile silence. He never mentioned that there weren't enough lifeboats for all the men on the tankers. Nor did he ally himself with the men who shipped out simply for room and board, like medieval tenant farmers. It was impossible for any tankerman—even Hal Banks—to kid himself about the romance of the sea, since most of his working life was spent on short, dirty hauls up and down the coast.

Banks' childhood was a painful topic, seldom mentioned. "The impression I got was that there were no happy memories," a Sailors' Union of the Pacific (SUP) officeworker recalls. And the few stories he told often conflicted. However, a history can be pieced together through court documents, newspaper accounts and conversations with family and acquaintances.

Harold Chamberlain Banks was born in Waterloo, Iowa, on February 28, 1909, the elder of two boys born to Herman A. Banks and the former Elsie Chamberlain—a surname he often adopted in his early criminal career. He did not maintain close contact with his family, although later in his life, after becoming a power in Canada, he would visit his father who by this time had moved to Los Angeles. Sometimes, Banks would say his father had owned land. Other times, he would say his father was the most crooked lawyer in all of Iowa. But the closest he came to expressing affection was the time he admitted respect for his father's toughness. Part of the reason for this may have been that Banks suspected he was not really his father's son. As Banks would later ask his friend Johnny Wilson, ''How do I know he's my father? How do I know that I'm not a bastard?''

Banks spoke little of his mother, except that she taught school and died violently. But Wilson's wife Tracey believes that Banks really loved his mother: ''He was heartbroken when she got killed. . . . Some young driver was going too fast and hit her. She was crossing the street and he hit her.'' Banks was a young man at the time, and when he went to the funeral, his father and brother George, an engineer for a small equipment manufacturer, were haggling about how they'd pay for the service. According to Banks, he paid the whole bill.

Banks would later claim that, as a young man, he had studied engineering at the University of California at Berkeley, after serving some time in the U.S. Navy. A check with the universities in the area shows no record of his attendance. However, records of a different kind show that by the time Banks had reached the age of twenty-one, he had appeared before a judge in Los Angeles, charged with issuing bad cheques. Those charges on July 22, 1930, were not his first. In March of that year, a similar charge resulted in his being placed on probation. But this time he was also accused of burglarizing a luxurious estate, and he refused to tell sheriffs anything about his accomplices. As a repeat offender, then Banks was sentenced by the judge to a maximum fourteen years in San Quentin for the cheque offences. Because of the severity of the sentence, the deputy district attorney asked for dismissal of the burglary charge.

After serving three and a half years in San Quentin, Banks was freed and headed back to the Richmond tankers. He had little to say about his prison time, except that he never wanted to return.

But on January 15, 1937, he was again before a judge. This time the charge was murder.

He was accused of kicking a man to death in a drunken Long Beach brawl. According to a witness at Nina's Cafe, Banks picked a fight with thirty-nine-year-old Oral Hammer of Long Beach at the 2:00 a.m. closing time. Hammer, an Anglo-American, had infuriated Banks by speaking Spanish to a night-club hostess. Fuelled by a long night's drinking with another sailor, Banks dared Hammer to go outside. When Hammer obliged, Banks knocked him to the ground and beat him senseless. Then he dragged Hammer's body into his car and drove away, the bloodied man's feet sticking out the car window. That's how Hammer was found that next day, dead from the beating. The car was parked near the Marine Terminal, where the tanker *Torres*, on which Banks was a boatswain, was docked. Police believed Hammer died sometime in the night, after no attempt was made to get him medical attention.

The witness, twenty-four-year-old night-club hostess Marie Ruth Richards, told police that Banks drove her to her hotel in San Pedro and told her to "keep her mouth shut." When the police arrested Bank aboard the *Torres*, he told a rambling story that failed to explain what had happened. His conviction seemed certain, but when his case eventually came to trial, he was found not guilty. Richards, the key witness against him, had mysteriously disappeared.

Six months later Banks' fortunes dipped so far that he was supplementing his income by driving a taxi. It would be five more years before his luck improved. Salvation came in the form of a job offer from the hulking Gunnar Hexum, an organizer for the Sailors' Union of the Pacific. In retrospect the event was ironic: here was Banks, the man who would become Canadian labour's most ardent right-wing crusader, being hired into union work by a former member of the radical Industrial Workers of the World party (known as the "Wobblies"). But apart from his teenage brush with extremism Hexum was regarded on the coast as embodying all that was good about the young union. At six foot three and 280 pounds, Hexum could more than handle himself; nevertheless, he preferred reasoning to brawling. Moreover, he had a reputation of being scrupulously honest and genuinely caring about the members of his union. Any of his workers caught padding his accounts or stealing were fired on the spot.

Banks was greatly impressed by Hexum when he boarded a tanker at Point Richmond in May 1941 and spoke of strength in numbers through unionism. Without hesitation, Banks joined the SUP, and began hanging around the union's Fifth Street office, eventually prompting Hexum to hire him into the union as an organizer. It was a decision that Hexum would come to regard as a low point in an otherwise distinguished career, for, as he soon realized, Hal Banks was an exceptionally strange and violent young man.

He and Banks would often make long drives along the California coast to recruit new members. More than once, Hexum would doze off in the front passenger seat, then be awakened by violent swerves of the car. It would be Banks amusing himself by trying to run over small animals he spotted along the roadside.

Another disturbing incident took place at the Charing Cross, a small bar in Richmond popular with sailors who couldn't afford better. The establishment had a cozy relationship with the SUP, so when the bartender thought a patron seemed ripe to join the union, he'd call in an organizer like Hexum. It was on one such occasion that Hexum was heading to the Charing Cross when, outside the bar, he spotted Banks and a couple of rough-looking companions.

Banks explained they were waiting to beat up a sailor belonging to the rival National Maritime Union (NMU) as soon as he left the Charing Cross. "Have you even talked to the guy?" Hexum asked. Banks replied that he hadn't. So Hexum went into the bar and approached the man. He was the sailor the bartender had called him about. The man was, as the bartender had said, eager to switch from the NMU to the SUP. And when Hexum offered him six months free membership, he was so happy he began sobbing for joy. Banks was almost as emotional when Hexum escorted the new convert past him, although for very different reasons. As Hexum recalls: "Banks was quite upset he didn't get a chance to beat him up."

Banks proved himself to be a racist as well as a bully. Blacks had been brought up to Richmond from the Deep South during the Second World War to work in shipbuilding yards. When the war ended, however, the blacks stayed. Many whites resented their new neighbours, and these racial tensions led some members of the SUP to sneer that the initials of the rival NMU stood for "Niggers, Mexicans and Undesirables." Former SUP organizer Stan Weir recalls one occasion where he heard some of his colleagues telling prospective candidates, "We got to get a white union in here." When Weir angrily confronted one of the organizers, the man said he had been dispatched by Hal Banks, who boasted of belonging to the Ku Klux Klan and packing a gun. Weir then remembers taking his complaint to SUP president Harry Lundeberg, only to be told that "the man's doing a good job for us over there and we have to overlook some of his faults."

Banks made a show of being a hard worker, although it was difficult to gauge how much was theatre and how much was substance. It was painfully clear, however, that he lacked the devotion of men like Hexum. Banks was more interested in the trappings of power. He was an uncommonly rakish dresser for the waterfront, delighting in the Homburg hat and shirt he wore around the office. Almost immediately after being hired, he had business cards printed.

Throughout the 1940s Banks had a dizzying stream of relationships. He was married to a Gertrude McLaughlin in 1941, but the marriage foundered quickly. A year later the couple made newspaper headlines in a messy child-snatching case. Apparently, Gertrude's daughter from a previous relationship had been placed in the custody of the father's family. When Banks and Gertrude scooped the baby up for an afternoon drive, they were charged with kidnapping, but the charges were eventually dropped.

By 1944, Banks and Gertrude had parted company, and Banks had married and divorced a woman named Adeline. There were also numerous trysts, many of a sordid nature. Many of these took place on the boat Banks owned, and to which he liked to invite women for a cruise. Once aboard, they'd have to choose between Banks' advances and swimming to shore. On more than one occasion, Banks would bed the wife of a fellow sailor as soon as her unsuspecting husband shipped out. Women who didn't succumb to his charm often were conquered by force. As Ed Turner, who worked with Banks in the 1940s, recalls, Banks was saved from rape charges more than once through the intervention of SUP head Harry Lundeberg. ''He was really a bully around women,'' Turner observes. ''He wouldn't think twice about hitting a woman on the street.''

Despite his lack of concern for most people, Banks did show inordinate loyalty to Lundeberg. While Banks didn't match Lundeberg's commitment to unionism, he did master his distinctive strut—the kind of short, choppy stride a man makes aboard a rolling ship, and not unlike a bantam rooster patrolling a henhouse. Soon Banks was doing it too, but with a more exaggerated swagger.

Men like Banks were a necessary evil for Lundeberg. The shippers had their goon squads and high-level connections, and rival communist union men were known to attack SUP members with baseball bats implanted with razor blades. Another communist trick was to urinate into a packet of lye, then throw it into an enemy's eyes. Other attacks on the union could be more subtle. On at least one occasion, Lundeberg's phone was tapped. But despite their need for combat soldiers, many in the SUP would have preferred that Lundeberg fire Banks.

During the late 1940s Banks transferred from the SUP to the broader-based Seafarers' International Union (SIU), which boasted coast-to-coast membership. With the broader base came entry into the rough Atlantic and Gulf areas, where mob connections took precedence over high idealism. The SIU needed muscle, not philosophers, and Banks fit the bill perfectly. Times were difficult, however. Banks was soon in danger of being laid off and sent back to sea. There was a general cutback in shipping and little work for organizers. Ed Turner, who shared Banks' office, did ship out again as a sailor.

Then Banks was picked for an assignment in Canada. No one else particularly wanted the job, nor did anyone think that it would last more than six months. Some union men joked that the job was first offered to someone else, who, upon arriving in Montreal in the middle of a snowstorm, cursed, climbed back on the plane, and flew home. Whether or not this was true, however, no one ever thought that Banks was being promoted to an administrative job. Banks was, after all, no more than a goon in a Homburg hat.

He had been a fink, sailing through the Standard Oil strike of the 1930s. The Standard Oil contract fiasco showed he could be seduced by shippers willing to massage his ego. His commitment to honest unionism was—at best—questionable. Each of these qualities made him attractive to Canadian shipping interests looking for someone brutal but pliable to do a dirty job, then go home.

"They knew he was a fink," said an old San Francisco Bay associate who didn't want to be identified. "They knew all of that up there. So they figured they'd get a sweetheart deal out of Banks. . . . They figured if a guy comes out of that type of background, they can use him up there. That's why they really helped him. They did everything they could for him up there."

Hal Banks seemed to be their man. But the shippers and others who brought Banks to Canada badly underestimated his all-consuming ambition.

3

I have been in jails and I have been on ships, and let me tell you, the condition in jails were far better than some of the vessels I sailed on.

Dan Daniels, former
Canadian Seamen's Union member

Banks wheeled his Buick into Montreal at the time when Canadian labour was split into the Canadian Congress of Labour and the Trades and Labor Congress, of which the Canadian Seamen's Union (CSU) was a member. More than half of TLC members also belonged to the U.S.-based American Federation of Labor. These American ties alternately added muscle to Canadian unions and threatened their autonomy. It was a delicate balance that Banks utterly ignored. If there were contradictions he would resolve them with bloodshed, not debate.

By early 1949 a costly, complicated labour situation had developed on the Great Lakes. The CSU had been involved in sixty-six strikes or work stoppages over the past year and tensions on the Lakes were multiplying. It was widely recognized that the CSU had had Communist party members in its top ranks since shortly after the union's formation in 1935 as the National Seamen's Union. Apologists are quick to make the distinction, however, that these were *Canadian* communists concerned with Canada and Canadian workers. Nevertheless, after the Second World War, the union had a new militancy and, critics argue, direct and tight Moscow control.

The average CSU sailor wasn't a communist—even if the average CSU leader was. The union was born in the Great Depression when a sailor was little better than a slave. Disgusting food, filthy cabins and unsafe conditions were the sailor's lot. When sailing in the tropics, he'd swelter below board because there weren't fans or adequate ventilation. During winter sailing, his toilet facilities might be a long, frozen trough in front of the sleeping quarters. Cranes that were needed to launch lifeboats often froze solid, giving him no escape in the event of a disaster.

Dan Daniels, former editor of the CSU newspaper, *The Searchlight*, remarks that sailors didn't need Moscow to tell them that conditions were appalling.

> I have been in jails and I have been on ships, and let me tell you, the conditions in jails were far better than some of the vessels I sailed on. Listen, in a jail—I was in jail as a seamen, as a trade unionist—I never had water leaking in on me. I never had steam pipes overhead my bunk. . . . Sometimes it gets so cold, if you're not thinking, your hand can freeze to the bulkheads. It's bloody cold, the water as it hits the side of the ship. The shipowners from the very beginning were thugs.
>
> Had there not been a Communist party in Canada, many of the seamen would have invented a revolutionary party of their own. The seamen were far more revolutionary and radical than any Communist party of Canada could have been. They were living in the most dire of situations, they were more class conscious—I would say—than most working people because there they were, working on the ships, and they knew they could never become a shipowner. And yet men who never worked on the ships, never had to toil, never had to sweat, never had to face submarines, never had to do any . . . dirty work . . . were becoming rich. We saw the conditions of people all over the world and that opened up our eyes. . . . When you saw men as I did in Panama . . . going into the garbage cans to take the food home for their families. Or you'd see little boys in the West Indies offering their sisters or their brothers or themselves to you. . . . If they [the sailors] became communists, it was not because of Moscow. They didn't care about Moscow.

With the CSU, sailors gained little things that brought dignity —such as better quality soap, lightbulbs above bunks and regular lifeboat drills—as well as better wages. A major victory was the eight-hour day. Before this, sailors would work twelve hours a day, seven days a week, in a constant, numbing cycle of six hours on the job and six hours rest.

The CSU was founded by a diminutive, ferret-eyed Irish immigrant named Pat Sullivan. Formerly a ship's cook, he set up the union's first office in Montreal in 1935. But the doors had scarcely opened before members of the Communist Party passed through them offering help. The new union had enthusiasm, momentum and a charter with the All-Canadian Congress of Labour (later to become the Canadian Congress of Labour after it merged with the Canadian section of the Congress of Industrial Organizations). What the new union lacked was money. A man who introduced himself as Mr. Dumbrovitch offered to help out. When he learned that Sullivan didn't draw a salary, Dumbrovitch handed him ten dollars. Further assistance came with the loan of a typewriter and provision of mimeographing services to publish leaflets. According to Sullivan, it was two months later that he realized Dumbrovitch was in fact Fred Rose, Quebec leader of the Communist Party of Canada.

Although it was gratitude that brought Sullivan to his first Communist Party meeting, the increasing intensity of his political convictions kept bringing him back. Mainstream labour seemed indifferent to the plight of the sailors, while the communists literally put clothing on Sullivan's back. Soon they were paying the salaries of Sullivan and an assistant and their travelling expenses. Decisions came to be undertaken jointly, such as the CSU's move away from the All-Canadian Congress of Labour towards the American Federation of Labor, and the public distancing of the CSU from the U.S.-based (and communist-controlled) National Maritime Union. It was a symbiotic relationship with immediate dividends for both sides: the union got funding and tactical expertise; the communists enjoyed a respectable entrée into mainstream labour.

Communist Party executive member J.B. Salzberg was delighted with the new arrangement: "Where else could the Communist Party get such a wonderful set-up? Here was a young organization with 1,200 members, whose delegates attend the central bodies of the labour movement, both in Montreal and in

Toronto. This enabled the delegates of the union to carry out the party line in the very heart of the labour movement.''

And so the ties between the union and communists tightened. Critics would charge they tightened to the point that the union's hands were soon tied. By the time Banks reached Canada, these ties were strangling the union.

Banks' arrival was preceded by further developments in Canadian Cold War politics with the strange revelations of a young Soviet cipher clerk in Ottawa named Igor Gouzenko. By offering proof that Soviet spying reached all the way into the House of Commons, Gouzenko helped foster a climate where the very worst was believed—and expected—of Moscow.

The spectre of the Red menace affected not only government and shippers, but certain labour leaders as well. Canadian Congress of Labour head Aaron Mosher often complained that he was ''doublecrossed every time he dealt with a Communist.'' The CCL dealt harshly with the post-war communist threat by purging itself of communist-dominated unions, including the International Union of Mine, Mill and Smelter Workers of America and the United Electrical Workers.

Within the TLC, the actions of the CSU were increasingly hard to defend. Even easy-going members of the TLC couldn't help wonder if the union hadn't become strike-happy and reckless after the Second World War. Nevertheless, it shocked Canadian unionists in March 1947 when a member of the CSU charged publicly that the union was communist-dominated—particularly since that man was none other than the union's president and founder, Pat Sullivan. No one had foreseen such a move. Sullivan was enormously popular within his union and had become secretary-treasurer of the TLC. But at the press conference he had called to make his charges public, he announced both his resignation from the CSU and the formation of the Canadian Lake Seamen's Union (CLSU).

Many CSU members blamed overwork and a taste for liquor for Sullivan's dramatic shift. Less charitable critics charged that he was paid off by shippers, and there is some evidence to support this. Captain Norman Reoch, operating manager of Canada Steamship Lines, and Scott Misener, president of Colonial Steamships Ltd. and Sarnia Steamships Ltd., had offered CSU secretary T. Gerald McManus $100,000 to set up a rival union. Also, according to CSU members, Sullivan had asked the union to help buy him a car shortly before his defection, but had been turned down. Not long after he quit the CSU, however, he had enough money to set up a hunting camp in the Gatineau Hills.

Whatever Sullivan's immediate motivation, the story of communist domination within the CSU was corroborated three years later by similar allegations from McManus. Formerly a Regina alderman, McManus was a long-time communist loyalist who joined the union in 1945 on orders from the Party, despite having no experience in either sailing or union work. He charged that CSU elections were a sham, with top officers picked by Communist party head J.B. Salzberg "with the offhand assurance of a baseball manager naming his starting line-up."

Not surprisingly, Canadian shipping companies flocked to the newly formed CLSU. Shortly after Sullivan's defection, Canada Steamship Lines, Colonial Steamships Ltd. and Sarnia Steamships Ltd. stopped honouring their contracts with the CSU in favour of Sullivan's new union. In response the CSU forged an agreement with the TLC, giving it power to act as the union's bargaining agent, thereby providing a more respectable front for negotiating with shippers. But the companies wouldn't budge.

In the spring of 1948, Industrial Inquiry Commissioners Leonard W. Brockington, Q.C. and J.D. McNish ruled the shippers weren't acting fairly:

> . . . it is our opinion that the failure to negotiate, the substitution of a new union for the existing bargaining unit and the assertion by the Company [Canada Steamship Lines] of the right to refuse to negotiate because of its objection to alleged political opinions are contrary to accepted practices and the law as it has heretofore been followed. We feel too, that in the result injustice has been done to the rank and

file of the Canadian Seamen's Union, particularly those to whom seniority rights have accrued.

Shippers ignored the report, and the climate of lawlessness worsened. Blood ran along the Great Lakes during the summer of 1948, as the CSU tried to shut down vessels manned by the upstart CLSU. At the same time, the CSU was striking to protest the shippers' refusal to bargain, which only strengthened the shippers' bond with the CLSU. Sullivan's presence on the waterfront infuriated his former union brothers in the CSU, who reacted with the passion of jilted lovers. At the same time, however, Sullivan's strong nationalism and desire for an independent Canadian union made his new allies uneasy and they looked south for support. By September 1948, the CLSU had merged with the Seafarers' International Union of North America (SIU), who had a tiny base on Canada's west coast. The move cut Sullivan out of the new order and brought the might of the SIU's parent federation, the American Federation of Labor (AFL) to the Canadian shores of the Great Lakes. Key matchmakers of the new relationship were officials from Canada Steamship Lines, Canada's largest shipper, and Frank Hall of the Brotherhood of Railway and Steamship Clerks, Freight Handlers, Express and Station Employees. Like Hexum a decade before, Hall would grow to deeply regret his sponsorship of Banks. By the early 1960s, Hall lived in fear that the man he helped bring to Canada would leave him dead in a ditch.

The TLC was furious, and accused the AFL of using bully tactics to meddle in a Canadian dispute. The AFL counterattacked that the TLC discriminated against members of American-based unions and harboured communists. The AFL's answer to communism was to be in the burly, violent personage of Hal C. Banks.

4

Let me tell you that uneasy lies the head that wears a crown.

Hal C. Banks

When Banks was sent to Montreal, he had a free hand, expert support, seemingly limitless funds and the mandate of wrenching control of the Great Lakes from the CSU. The exact amount of money that Banks brought to Canada is unclear. At one point, he bragged that he had $100,000 in his war chest. At another point, he placed the figure at $500,000. However much it was, there was certainly enough for Banks to buy out all the baseball bats and bicycle chains in a Montreal Eaton's store before one day's hostilities. Not surprisingly, violence escalated.

As Dan Daniels recalls:

> We had an informer come to us in Montreal in 1949. He had tried to work both sides. He had just had a meeting. He gave us a record of the meeting which included people from the strikebreaking organization and the police—whether this was true or not I do not know. But he said to us, ''You, Danny Daniels, you will be killed. You will be dumped in the water. And it has been agreed that when you are pulled out of the water, your death will be assumed to be from intoxicating influences.'' That was the verdict of three of our men who were killed in San Francisco . . . The only strongmen we had were our own members. We had no hired men.

In the spring and summer of 1949, the CSU led a series of dock strikes in England that resulted in the loss of 400,000 work days —and the life of the CSU. The union was now fighting for far bigger stakes than light bulbs over bunks and decent food. The

Second World War had ended with Canada owning the third largest merchant fleet in the world. However, with Liberal Prime Minister Louis St. Laurent and Department of Reconstruction head C.D. Howe determined to reconvert Canada's economy from wartime controls to free enterprise, Ottawa was now selling off publicly owned ships to foreign interests for bargain-basement prices. Canadian ships were simply too slow, inefficient and costly to compete in postwar shipping. Now ships purchased by Canadian taxpayers were registered under the flags of the Bahamas, Panama and Greece. No longer did they have to honour the wage rates and conditions won by the CSU.

When the CSU announced that it was fighting back in 1949 by striking at deep-sea ports around the world, Ottawa accused the union of complicity in a Soviet plot to tie up the Marshall Plan and its aid to war-ravaged Europe. A world strike would be an enormous propaganda victory for the communists. McManus charged that the strike came at the secret request of the British Communist Party, which hoped that such an action would snap British workers into new militancy.

Harry Davis, appointed CSU head by the Canadian Communist Party, called the charges of Moscow-ordered strikes "a lot of garbage." Davis, born Harry Popovich, claims that he offered to step down during the strike because of the communist issue. "We were prepared to go back to work under the conditions of the previous contract," he recalls. "Does that sound like somebody who wanted to go on strike and sabotage the Marshall Plan?"

But McManus argues that Davis was bent on paralysing deep-sea traffic and "called the strike without even going through the empty formality of consulting the union executive or asking for a vote from the members." McManus described Davis as "beside himself with elation" at the onset of the 1949 strike, declaring, "We can strike the world!" According to McManus, the strike was "tactically insane" for the CSU and effectively "sealed its doom."

Four decades later, the sudden, violent death of the CSU is still an emotionally charged topic. Former CSU members still deeply resent being portrayed as communist dupes. Many had been lionized as heroes for their courage on the North Atlantic during the Second World War, only to be blacklisted as communists when they returned home. Former CSU patrolman Joe Grabek still bristles at questions about Moscow control of his union:

> Nobody wanted a strike. We were forced into it. . . . Nobody in his right mind is looking for a strike. But if they kick you in the ass, you're not going to bend over and have them kick you again. . . . We just wanted to be in decent working conditions, instead of being looked on as a bunch of goddamned animals. We wanted to be human beings . . . .
>
> The seamen were the union. No one else. It was the seamen. There was nobody else. You stuck together. You had no choice but to stick together. Otherwise, you were treated like an animal. . . . Christ, we didn't even know how to spell Moscow. We did not know where it was. At least the majority of us . . .
>
> We wanted to maintain a fleet under the Canadian flag. That's going back to the experience of what happened after the First World War . . . when Canada got rid of the fleet. . . . Conditions get worse. Not only that. It's a disadvantage to Canada economically. Look at the jobs that are lost in the shipyards, maintenance, the seamen. Not only that, but Canada is paying through the nose to foreign shipowners to carry her cargo. As a trading nation, we should have a fleet to carry our goods. . . . We were fighting for Canada. As Canadians, we were fighting for Canada. We would not sell out to the U.S. like our government did.

Banks was clearly the Canadian government's man. Mounties lined the Seaway to protect SIU-manned ships and escorted strikebreakers as they replaced CSU crews. The last gasp of the CSU was in Halifax in April, when the SIU crewed Canadian National Steamship (CNS) ships that had been under contract to the CSU. Shotgun blasts were fired down onto the CSU strikers and the ships sailed out of Halifax, taking with them hopes of the union ever recovering.

The CSU was bloodied in the conference room as well as on the waterfront. The SIU pressured other AFL-affiliated international unions belonging to the TLC to withhold from it their per-capita dues payments. By May 1949, the TLC was faced with the threat of losing dues from 100,000 members. There was also the fear that these workers might form a rival, AFL-backed Congress. The CSU was proving to be a costly embarrassment to the TLC. At best, it was misguided. Its world strike had alienated mainstream Canadian unionists and played into the hands of the SIU and shippers. So it came as no surprise when, in June 1949, the battered Canadian Seamen's Union was cut adrift by the TLC and left to die alone.

Banks' speech to his American cohorts in March 1951 reveals the extent of the campaign against the CSU:

> The Canadian Seamen's Union resorted to violence such as has never been witnessed in a labor war. Wholesale mayhem and attempted murder were the order of the day. We were forced by the circumstances to meet this deplorable situation with the only thing that these people can understand and that was the same thing that they were giving us, with interest. . . . It is needless for this report to go into the events at Halifax, Saint John, Welland, Fort William, Vancouver, Victoria and Montreal. We would choose to just say that the battles were many and although the Seafarers' International Union did not always win the first round, we won the majority of these battles decisively . . . .
>
> The Atlantic and Gulf District of the Seafarers' International Union of North America and the Sailors' Union of the Pacific gave all-out aid, morally, financially and physically, particularly [official Morris] Weisberger came into Halifax with a group of experts and fought a battle that they will remember. They brought in specialists in certain fields. They brought in men who knew their business when it came to drawing up transcripts for radio broadcasts, they brought in experts in public relations and they brought in broad shouldered boys—in fact, a complete setup.

From the CSU perspective, Daniels acknowledges his union was outgunned: "There was nothing that we could do to stop the SIU because it had the support of the government. The government would not allow us to survive. Period. We had become, as far as they were concerned, too much of a threat. And they would not let us survive—no more so than Moscow could allow [Polish trade union] Solidarity to survive."

For Banks it was a heady time. Just a year earlier he had been facing the prospect of being sent back to sea. Now he had donned the mantle of fearless anti-communist crusader and was treated with respect by government, police, wealthy shippers and the elite of his union. He packed his pistol with the blessing of the Canadian government. He was being told what he had always felt—that he was a great man. How much tougher could it be to become the top labour leader in Canada or even Prime Minister? On April 27, 1949, his ambition bubbled feverishly in a letter to Carol Banks, the SIU officeworker in San Francisco whom he was then calling his wife.

> My Dear Darling:
>
> Am ashamed as usual but you know how it is. Never been swept up in such a large operation before and it sure is taxing everything I have, but I am winning hands down and will soon be in the dubious possition [*sic*] of being the top labor man in all of Canada. But let me tell you that uneasy lies the head that wears a crown. Have not even had time to get my socks from the customs house. Wish I could get you up here right away but you would not enjoy it here now as I would only see you about ten minutes a day. I have a little tank of fish in my office. I enjoy them. I am well and safe so don't worry about me as you know that I find my way around alright [*sic*] and take good care of myself.
>
> We have the full cooperation of the police and I have a permit to carry a gun.
>
> We have manned most of the ships and the money is just rolling in so everything is fine.
>
> Hope you were not as disapointed [*sic*] as I was at my having to postpone the trip but it is the only thing to do just

now but I hope to change it soon. Always remember that I love you very dearly and always will.
Your Hal.

Banks and Carol were together again in June 1950. The occasion was the official opening of the Sailors' Union hall in San Francisco. The hall, designed by noted architect William Gladstone Merchant, is in the art deco style, and succeeds in bringing to mind the grace of a ship in full sail: the columns create the illusion of sails; its portico, the illusion of a foredeck.

The building stands on Rincon Hill, midway between the financial district and the wharves, and serves as a hiring hall and recreation centre. It is fittingly within view of one of the union's great moral victories, the bloody battle of 1934 when two unionists were killed in street fighting with police.

For Harry Lundeberg, the building was a proud symbol of his union's progress. He bragged that the $1,500,000 structure was "the finest union building in the world" and dedicated it to American sailors killed during the Second World War keeping supply lines open for Allied troops. In addition to inviting a who's who of California society to its official opening—including Governor Earl Warren—Lundeberg invited Hal Banks, fresh from his Canadian victory. He returned a conquering hero, having crushed the communists and signed over leading shippers, including the largest in the nation, Canada Steamship Lines.

Tea and sandwiches were served, although guests could also draw from a healthy supply of spirits. Many did, as eighty-eight cases of whisky were opened and consumed that afternoon and Banks, who had been having troubles with Carol, certainly had his fair share. Word was that he had staged a phony marriage ceremony with Carol in Portland. And while the reasons aren't clear, one can imagine that Banks tricked her into thinking she was married to him. Now she was complaining that Banks had beaten her and she approached her friend Jack Casper, hoping he could persuade Banks to stop.

Casper, a former pro boxer and future bodyguard for Teamster president Dave Beck, stood six foot six and weighed somewhere between 270 and 295 pounds; he was known as a powerful puncher. But it appears that Casper's reputation didn't faze Banks during the opening that afternoon. He baptised the new union hall by brawling with Casper. As one witness recalls, ''Banks was not afraid of nobody at any time; he wouldn't care who you were, what you were.''

But Banks' spunk didn't match Casper's right hand. ''Casper just struck his fist up his belly about as far as his arm would go, and that was the end of it.''

Another man might have held a grudge, but Banks knew talent when he saw—and felt—it. His relationship with Carol wouldn't last but it wasn't too long before he had Casper up in Montreal on his payroll.

5

Our men are at sea most of the time. They're away from home, alone. They've got to feel that somebody loves them and is looking after them. That's where we come in.

Hal Banks describes the role of the Seafarers' Union

Banks had an instinctive need to dominate everything and everyone around him. Finally, at age forty, he was in control and there was no way he planned to return to California. Montreal was now his home.

At that time, Montreal was a city of brothels and basilicas, where the urges of the flesh commanded the same careful attention as the sacraments for the soul. In the shadows of the stone churches were some two hundred bordellos, along with a mixed bag of gambling houses and ''blind pigs''—the street term for illegal drinking spots.

Few servicemen complained about being stationed in Montreal during the Second World War, although the port caused their superiors some concern. Venereal disease picked up along the Main became such a problem that the military commandant for the Montreal area threatened to make the entire city off limits if something wasn't done.

But the city's underworld was in fine health when the war ended. And when later crusaders tried to clean things up, they faced opposition not just from the crime community, but also from compromised civic and provincial politicans, newspapermen, police and the judiciary. Corruption also extended to a large portion of the Montreal press, which had come to regard payoffs as its just due. When the Duplessis era finally ended, there were moanings in the Montreal Press Club. Reporters wondered how they could manage without their regular envelopes of bills from the provincial government.

There had been a spirited attempt at reform in Montreal in 1946. But its leaders soon discovered the number of friends the city's top criminals had in respectable society. A few years later, the Ligue d'Action Civique, led by young lawyer Jean Drapeau, would learn the same thing.

In 1950, Drapeau and his flamboyant boss Pacifique Plante demanded a public inquiry into corruption. Their demands were backed by a 1,095-page report that catalogued 15,000 charges. Among them: the practice of enumerating dogs and cats for elections; brass-knuckled goons brawling at polling stations; and at least one incident where a police morality-squad leader was found issuing condoms to his men before a raid on a bordello.

The Caron Commission of the early 1950s would again try, largely in vain, to clean things up. But with the Kefauver hearings in the U.S. Senate driving mafiosi such as Carmen Galente to Montreal, the task was even more difficult. Galente, second-in-command to New York City gang boss Joe Bonanno, has been elegantly described by co-authors Brian McKenna and Susan Purcell in *Drapeau* as "a ruthless Sicilian killer who had the manners of a Vanderbilt, the reputation of a diplomat and the ambition of Al Capone."

It wouldn't be long before Hal Banks would be compared to Capone as well. He had won the war with the Canadian Seamen's Union. Now he could roll into the office of a Cabinet minister or a shipper like Canada Steamship Lines' Rodgie McLagan as if he owned it. He knew all their phone numbers by memory and when he called them, he was never put on hold. Shippers and government officials didn't seem to mind the crude newcomer because their ships were moving again. One shipper read perfectly the fusion of corruption and ambition that was Banks. He gave Banks a large globe on a mahogany stand for his office. When Banks pressed a button on the brass panel beside his desk, the globe popped open and revealed a fully stocked bar.

Many union men did mind Banks' continued presence but that didn't seem to matter. Most had no real alternative to working for him. The coup de grâce had been dealt to the CSU by the Canada Labour Relations Board on December 7, 1950, when a certification with one shipper, Branch Line Limited, was revoked on the grounds that the CSU was no longer a trade union because it was communist-controlled and -directed.

Banks offered sailors himself as a symbol of power at the same time as he made them virtually powerless within their own union. He spoke of power in absolute terms with the clear assumption that every man in his union was behind him no matter what he did or where he wanted to go. Those officeworkers who weren't enthusiastic followers found themselves branded as deadwood and fired. Sailors who weren't willing to live under Banks' laws were blacklisted from their jobs.

Before Banks came to Canada, blacklisting was a common practice among shippers who wanted to prevent troublesome sailors from shipping out on their vessels. And Banks was more than willing to ingratiate himself with the shippers by continuing this corporate tradition. When he signed a contract with Canada Steamship Lines in 1949, he agreed not to ship out some eighty sailors who were listed in the company's bad books. Soon afterwards, Banks took over the blacklisting function himself. To hear him explain it, however, good union men had nothing to fear from the Do Not Ship (DNS) list. It was just for "Commie agitators, epileptics, sleepwalkers, perverts, drunks and thieves." Little did the sailors know that, by 1956, the estimated size of the DNS list would be at least 6,000 names—mostly of men whose only crime consisted of doing something that might make Hal Banks' life less comfortable. That could include complaining about insects in the food served to sailors on vessels run by a favoured shipper or pushing for democracy within the union. Sailors were placed on the DNS list without trial and weren't told the charges that cost them their jobs.

The threat of the DNS list also meant that Banks had no trouble manning picket lines. Banks' men simply confiscated union cards and permits before sending the men to the lines. Cards were returned when picketing was over. The choice was simple: picket or don't work.

To those who followed the Banks line, he was "Papa Hal"—a strict, but benevolent father figure. Banks instinctively realized the importance of such symbols. He presented himself as the embodiment of new-found power for sailors, that people who once looked down on sailors might now respect and even fear them.

Before Banks, Vancouver SIU members met in a dingy downtown walkup, where they had to go four doors down the street to use washroom facilities in a Chinese laundry. Now SIU halls were something to be proud of. The Montreal hall was even luxurious. Between its green, mock-marble panels, a sailor could get a shoeshine, a cheap meal, medical attention, a free haircut, use the union library or play pool. It was a clean, orderly environment—and kept that way with the help of a separate set of sawed-off, club-size pool cues that were kept under the dispatch counter on the first floor.

"Remember," Banks would say, "when these fellows blow into town the lieutenant-governor doesn't invite them over. It's our job to make them comfortable. Our men are at sea most of the time. They're away from home, alone. They've got to feel that somebody loves them and is looking after them. That's where we come in."

Traditionally, Canadian sailors had not formed allegiances to particular companies. Loyalty was to their friends, many of whom migrated from the same regions for the same reasons—to supplement incomes from farming or fishing. In turn, shippers were often indifferent or hostile to sailors. Little effort was made to upgrade sailors' skills or provide them with welfare schemes. It wasn't unusual for sailors to be abandoned in foreign ports, replaced by cheaper foreign workers.

Geography also discouraged bonding with companies. It took less than a month to make a return voyage through the entire Great Lakes, so sailors constantly moved from ship to ship and company to company.

Banks offered the sailors something to bond with, however. He forced his way into the centre of their working lives and struggled to make them see his successes as their successes. When he bought a new Cadillac each year, he said it was for the image of their union. The same applied to the extravagant numbers of suits and shirts that he had made. Fittings were often undertaken at the office, while union officials and office visitors looked on.

Papa Hal loved to boast about the efforts that he and his staff made to look after his boys. An example he used was of one sailor who had complained that his landlord had locked him out of his apartment and confiscated his radio and clothes. All Banks had to do, so the story goes, was to "phone and explain that the reason he [the sailor] raised hell the night before was that he's been at sea for two months and can't hold his beer. I ask him to give the boy his stuff back and he'll leave quietly."

A story Banks would be less likely to mention might be how he promised legal help for another Seafarer who was charged with attempted murder in 1949. The man had accompanied Banks to Halifax at the height of the CSU war, and was charged after firing a shotgun into a crowd of rival union men. Banks promised to help him out. But when the man's court date came, Banks was in bed with the prisoner's wife. And if she thought she was paying Banks to help her husband, she soon found out how mistaken she was. The man went to prison when Banks reneged on his promise to provide a lawyer. Even after his release, he never worked for the union again.

Any magnanimity that Banks showed to his union members was usually reserved for when he had an audience. On one occasion, according to a rival union officer who was in his office at the time, Banks was approached by a distraught sailor's wife who was begging for help. Her husband had been injured and the family was penniless. Was there something in the union's welfare plan that could help her? With no reporters in the office, Banks just laughed.

"You just want to get fucked," he chortled, his laughter chasing her as she fled the hall.

6

White Knight on a Cadillac

Headline in *The Financial Post*

Some people objected to the presence of the elegant stone house at 95 Lakeshore Road in Pointe Claire, a community lying just southeast of Montreal. In fact, even before Hal Banks took possession of the house, it had been the centre of some controversy. Like Banks, people said it didn't belong. It sat right on the edge of Lac Saint Louis, blocking the view of the water for neighbours across the street. There were grumblings that zoning regulations had been broken to allow it there. Not that that would have disturbed Banks. Immediately after moving in, he began work to double the size of the house by building an addition at the back. Landscaping was done and trees were planted. Union funds paid to dredge the dock and work was done by union men being paid for another job.

Nevertheless, Banks worked just as hard at being a model neighbour. When his gofer-cum-bodyguard, Roman Gralewicz, littered another homeowner's lawn, Banks shouted angrily at him to pick up the mess. As former neighbour Donald Crichton recalls, "He didn't want any bad neighbourly relations. . . . This was his haven. Around here he had peace."

It was difficult to square the Hal Banks of Lakeshore Road with the image of Hal Banks the waterfront despot. The first time Crichton met him, Banks was wandering about, hunting for his prize pet Siamese cat. Crichton had just buried a Siamese cat that had been hit by a car. When he told Banks about the accident, "He was quite distraught . . . visibly upset. Really, he held this cat in such high affection." The two men struck up a conversation and Banks invited Crichton in, cheered somewhat by the chance to show off his new home.

As Crichton remembers, "it was absolutely spotless. I said, 'Hal, do you feel a bit exposed with [all] those windows? People . . . are going to want to take a shot at you.' He said, 'No sonofabitch ever tangled with me.' Right behind the curtain there's a big rifle, loaded. He said, 'I'm an expert shot.' " (According to other neighbours, Banks also had a telescope mounted in a window overlooking Lac Saint Louis, so he could spot enemies approaching by water.)

Banks claimed to be an expert at almost everything. And he was an expert at many things, including lying, so Crichton was often left wondering what was fact and what was fantasy. He told of sailing races in which he raced windjammers from California to Hawaii (naturally, he was the skipper). He bragged of having an international reputation as a cook as well.

Crichton recalls one of his experiences as Banks' dinner guest. "It was just remarkable the way he had prepared supper. Again, he was an expert at it. He said, 'I have tenderloin hamburgers.' As he was preparing it, I was watching him. . . . There was never any mess. No junk, no dirty dishes, no garbage. I don't know how he did it. When he sat down to eat, it was spotless. . . . "

After complimenting him on his culinary skill, Crichton remembers that Banks launched into a story. The twin cities of Minneapolis and St. Paul decided to have a hundredth-anniversary celebration. They called on him to prepare the food for both cities.

> . . . Maybe it was a pack of lies. He said that he had the bulldozers dig a trench, I don't know how many hundred yards long. . . . Then he put coals into it and then he covered the coals with sand or something and had I don't know how many dozens of hogs or turkeys or sheep carcasses put in there, and then backfilled. This was a week before the thing and they just cooked there.
>
> He was proud to tell me that the day of this big feast, they opened up this big grave and took everything out. He said, the food was just perfect. All the meat was done to a turn and everybody thought he was a hero class one.

Whatever his neighbour's qualifications as a civic caterer may have been, Crichton didn't doubt that Banks was a technical wizard. On one occasion Banks pulled apart the Cadillac engine that he'd had installed in his motor launch and found that it had been made to only average specifications—not to the special standards he had ordered. He sent it back to the company and received a replacement with the custom modifications.

Crichton was also amazed by Banks' inventive use of new technology: "He bought one of those electroencephalograph gimmicks with the things that check your heart. . . . This was years ago when these things came out, to check the efficiency of the motor. He said, 'You know, I couldn't be satisfied watching this thing run. I had to take it all apart.' So he had this electronic gadget all apart and put it back together. And that satisfied him."

Banks actually had two boats at home, a cabin cruiser and a speedboat. Word at the union hall was that one day on the lake he was passed by a faster speedboat. After this, he bought an even faster one—paid for, as was all of Banks' personal fleet, with union funds. When someone pointed this out to Banks, he snapped back that he wasn't charging the union rent for use of his personal dockspace.

When Banks felt like tinkering, he'd ensconce himself in his $15,000 home workshop, fully equipped with a lathe and all the best tools on the market. Gadgetry fascinated him. He loved to have things done for him at the push of a button. Buttons didn't talk back and could be programmed to do almost everything. Banks installed buttons to open and close his curtains, turn his hidden lawn sprinklers on and off, as well as activate the intercom at the front door. There were even buttons to control his automatic vegetable hamper, so the lord of the Seaway needn't strain to reach for his potatoes.

For Banks, the ultimate in auto engineering was the Cadillac Eldorado convertible. An article about Banks in *The Financial Post* was headlined "White Knight on a Cadillac." While the headline was ironic, it captured Banks' self-image. He cut a swashbuckling figure as he cruised up to the house in his white Eldorado, pushed a button to open the remote-controlled garage door and drove in. Back in the 1950s, few people besides Banks' neighbours knew such devices existed outside of the movies.

His Cadillacs had to be perfect. When faulty windshield wipers triggered an electrical failure, Banks replaced the entire car. Then there was the time he squashed the hood of another Eldorado by leaping out an upstairs window during a fire. That car was also replaced. And once, he found that the dealer from whom he bought a new Cadillac had put his metal crest on the back. Furious, he went back to the dealer and demanded to know who had done this. When the salesman responsible foolishly suggested that it would be an asset to have the plaque on his car, Banks "took that sonofabitch by the shoulders and . . . put him up on the desk and . . . said, 'One more smart remark out of you and you're dead! Now, I'll have a new Cadillac. Don't just take that plaque off. I want a new Cadillac and I want it now.' " Naturally, he got it. Years later, he would brag that he had owned thirty-three Cadillacs in his lifetime.

In one sense, Banks' fascination with mechanical things reflected his approach to human beings. People were like machinery. You analysed their component parts, then calculated how to make them do your bidding. If they responded to your commands quickly and efficiently, they deserved respect. If not, you trashed them and found something that did work.

Just as he enjoyed showing off his expensive possessions to neighbours like Crichton, Banks delighted in dropping the names of the important people he knew. Rodgie McLagan, head of Canada Steamship Lines, was a good guy, Banks would say. So was the headwaiter at the Queen Elizabeth. No matter how many people were waiting in line, Banks bragged that he just had to show his face to get a first-class table immediately. The prudish John Diefenbaker was a different matter, and Banks had no use for his prairie morality and refusal to wheel and deal. But on the whole, Banks devoted considerable energy to making and sustaining as many high-level contacts as possible. To assist in this, he would entertain lavishly at his Lakeshore Road home.

In the basement, Banks had constructed a recreation room with a decor that matched his penthouse office, with padded green imitation leather walls offset by shiny brass studs. It didn't look natural but it did look expensive. The doors had the same finish, and were padded so thickly it was tough to find the doorknobs, even if you wanted to leave.

There was also a massive bar that would have done a nightclub proud. It was stocked with cases of Crown Royal, champagne, gin and Black Label Scotch whisky, paid for with SIU funds and delivered by union workers.

''Well, you know I don't drink very much,'' Banks would say. ''But if these clowns around here expect me to entertain MPs and shipowners on their behalf, they are going to have to buy the liquor.''

The shipowners and MPs were apparently glad to be invited. They sipped fine liquor, listened to Mantovani on Banks' state-of-the-art sound system and, if so inclined, watched pornographic movies at a time when they were considered exotic and naughty. According to some reports, however, the camera equipment tucked into the wall was set up to serve another purpose. It could also be used to film those who partook of the top-grade hookers often present.

SIU vice-president Ed Turner recalls that he had no direct knowledge of the widely repeated stories that Banks had used hookers to blackmail politicians, shippers and rival unionists. On the other hand, he says, ''If you're talking the same thing Rockefeller used to do in New York, I suppose everybody did it. That's not anything unusual at all. . . . I know that they did it then. They do it today. . . . That's a way of business. . . . It depends on the weakness of the individual he's doing business with.''

While the residents of Lakeshore Road would not have seen what went on in the basement, whispers around the neighbourhood were that Banks had prostitutes stage fashion shows on his back terrace to impress influential guests. Women who applied for work with the Seafarers' often found their interview scheduled for Banks' home.

''One day I was getting in my car and going to the village and I saw a girl sitting on the cement over there in front of the steps,'' Crichton recalls. ''And I came back later and I was heading on into town and she was still sitting there. This was before there was any bus service. I stopped and I said, 'Are you in trouble? Do you want to go into town?' She said, 'Oh I would appreciate it very much.' She had a foreign accent. She got into the car and she was trembling. She said, 'You wouldn't believe the night I went through. Mr. Banks! He got me to come out here to stay for the night and what he was trying to do to me! Oh! I finally escaped from him. I went outside. He didn't follow me but I have no money and I don't know where to go. There was no taxis.' She was just petrified."

Although a steady flow of women was a standard feature of the Banks' household, some stayed longer than others. Carol, to whom Banks was allegedly married when he first came to Canada, left him in the early 1950s. Next he married Helen Lavigne, a proper Maritime woman, in Baltimore in 1953. But like Carol Banks, she too was beaten, and she too left him. Years later, she would provide her ex-husband's rivals with details of his financial misdealings, charging that he had siphoned off union funds and deposited them in U.S. bank accounts.

Next came Josie Charlebois, and it was she whom the Crichtons knew and liked. Charlebois was a slim, self-contained, dark-eyed French-Canadian beauty. She stayed with Banks in the late 1950s, ostensibly as his live-in nurse to tend to a back ailment. Wags noted that she had no nursing qualifications and that Banks' back problems were probably caused—not cured—by his parade of women.

Banks would often call Charlebois "the tigress." And according to guests at Banks' home, the name suited her. The occasion was Christmas dinner and Charlebois had brought the turkey in from the kitchen. It was beautifully browned, like something out of a picture. Banks started to carve, then dug out some stuffing and tasted it.

"That's fucking pigshit!" he spat. "What did you put in here?"

"I did what you told me," Charlebois said.

"That's not chestnuts!"

"Oh, I forgot the name of the nuts. You wanted chestnut dressing. I got Brazil nuts."

The Brazil nuts had broken down under the heat and the stuffing looked like goo. Banks was livid and started calling her every name he could think of. Responding with even greater fury, Charlebois grabbed the turkey as if to throw it at him. Then she ran out into the kitchen and began smashing all the dishes she could find.

Banks jumped up from the table and ran into the living room. When he came back with his handgun, he was taking the bullets out of it. Putting the gun in his pocket, he remarked "the fucking bitch will kill me one of these days if she gets to this before I do."

In later years, Banks took up with Marija Guchich, a sharp-featured, attractive Croatian immigrant several decades younger than he was. An excellent cook, she was a skilled hostess for Banks' powerful dinner guests. Most importantly, she was the mother of his daughter Sylvia, the one lasting female relationship of his life.

Neighbours also got a glimpse of a woman in her late teens who dropped by occasionally. Banks tersely explained that she was his daughter and that her mother and Banks weren't on friendly terms. One imagines it was the daughter of Gertrude McLaughlin, his wife of a decade before in Richmond.

Both Josie and Marija needed considerable patience to live with Banks. They had to weather his innumerable flings with prostitutes, officeworkers, and women easily impressed with his money, power and crude confidence. Years later, researchers for rival unions would try to dig up dirt on Banks by interviewing former girlfriends. Their list for 1957 alone included twenty-two names.

For all the stories Crichton heard, Banks was always friendly to him. One day Crichton decided to mix friendship with business, and he asked Banks if he could help him with a second mortgage on his home. Banks had been bragging about how he had bullied a bank into a sweet deal by threatening to withdraw SIU funds. Banks' reply was unequivocal: "I've got it. You can have it, but don't take it. I'm a good friend and neighbour with you, but when it comes to money, I'm a sonofabitch. Let's stay friends." Crichton took this as an odd gesture of friendship; the Banks of Pointe Claire had shielded him from the Banks of the waterfront.

7

The communists in our field are still lying dormant, and are eagerly awaiting the day when they can once again, through the democracy of our constitution, infiltrate into our ships, and set them up as hotbeds of dissension and sabotage. Some are within our ships already.

Banks supporter Leonard ''Red'' McLaughlin addresses sailors in 1951

Hal Banks didn't need special occasions to remind him that he was a powerful, successful man. He was reminded every time he slipped on one of his handmade suits, sat behind the wheel of a new Caddy convertible, or blacklisted a sailor from working for life. But it was still nice to hear others reinforce what he already knew. So when the SIU scheduled its biennial convention in Montreal for January 1951, Banks couldn't help feeling a special rush of pride.

Only two years earlier he had been on the verge of being laid off from his union job in California. Now the communists had been routed from the Great Lakes and most shippers were both comfortably and tightly stuffed into his pocket. It hadn't been pretty getting these results but he had got them. Hal Banks was given a tough job and he had done it. Even his enemies had to admit he was an effective organizer.

Banks wanted his convention guests to enjoy his new city. To help the out-of-towners, he drafted a tourist brochure that said as much about Banks as it did about Montreal.

''DO NOT PROCLAIM THAT YOU ARE A STRANGER IN TOWN,'' Banks warned in his brochure's section, ''Taxi Tips Around Town.'' ''ACT SELF-ASSURED AND AS THOUGH YOU ARE SURE OF WHERE YOU ARE GOING (even if you're not).''

Describing the Plaza Hotel, Banks wrote: ''If you want to get soused in an ungentlemanly manner, here it is. But even here they draw the line and call forth the bouncers. The ''line'' is judged by how well you have tipped. Many of our members fondly regard this vicinity as the place they were rolled for the first time. Not recommended if you don't want to be bothered by dames. A lot of loose gals here, some of whom have combined the finer things of life with the grim necessity of making a living. DON'T SAY WE DIDN'T LEVEL.''

No one could accuse Banks of also not levelling about Drury's Restaurant: ''Montrealers who like an occasional nip of the English atmosphere always head for Drury's. Along with the atmosphere comes the Limey ideas of 'dignity', and neither impromptu hula dances nor vocal imitations of Perry Como are appreciated.''

No so at the York Hotel: ''It's rough here. The wimmen [*sic*] are unspecified, and some have souvenirs to give away. The floor show is usually raw. Even the bartenders call the place a 'joint'. It is alleged that many of the gals use this joint as their place of business, and the price of their favours take what the traffic will bear. Let's face it . . . if you wind up here, you've left your inhibitions at home.''

For ''steaks and frolic'' at a more sedate pace, Banks recommended the Bellevue Casino: ''The expense account won't stand too many evenings at this pace, but the Missus (if you've brought her along) will love it.''

Banks noted the Cafe Copacabana also offered steaks and frolic. But while he praised its drinks and service, he questioned the ambiance: ''There are some nasty rumours amongst Montrealers that the 'Violet' set hang out here. That Liberace's music is referred to in honeyed tones. That may be a well may be [*sic*], the 'girls' have to have some place to go, and we can't blame the club for it. For those who hope to have the mailing address of some petite little French gal, the prospects here are as good as any.''

There was also a warning about the patrons of the Montmartre, a Harlem-style nightspot with a progressive tone: ''Those of us who hail from the Antarctic side of the Mason-Dixon line generally choke on the first drink at this spot. This is the headquarters for Montreal's coloured folk, and there's lots of 'em here. Sometimes their white gal friends, too. The Limeys freed the slaves a long time back, Canada sheltered the runaways from the States before 1812, and there is no segregation in Canada. Those who are broadminded in this respect will have a good evening here; those who have firm opinions on the subject question will do well to steer clear.''

Banks would have liked to impress Harry Lundeberg with his operation and his city, but his old boss said that he couldn't attend. He wired his regrets that he was busy with union business in Washington the entire week.

Montreal's Falstaffian mayor Camillien Houde also couldn't make it. He was tied up in a traffic meeting and sent as his representative Claude Jodoin, vice-president of the Trades and Labour Congress of Canada and president of the Montreal Trades and Labour Council. It wasn't what Banks had hoped for, but he gave Jodoin a hero's welcome none the less, and introduced him to the delegates as the man who ''in the dark days when the various Commie controlled unions in Canada were really shooting at us for the kill, . . . stood right alongside of us and took it on the chin with us when we were loosing.''

Jodoin reciprocated with a self-deprecating patter that led to a testimonial of his appreciation for Banks' work. Jodoin explained how Banks had lent muscle to an organizing drive for workers in the International Ladies' Garment Workers' Union:

> We had a terrific organizational campaign going on to organize the balance of the unorganized in the district of New York under our jurisdiction. So, lo and behold, according to our information at least, some of the manufacturers decided to go back to the days of ''Murder Incorporated''. If you don't know about that situation, you all have heard of ''Murder Incorporated''. They had gangsters and thugs and nice boys of that type and even went to the extent that they killed one of our own organizers. Now you can realize that the girls on the picket lines facing such type of gangsterism were not in the most interesting situation. So, without asking for it, the representative of the Seafarers' International Union in New York, offered their [*sic*] services to help the girls picket those shops which were on strike. I don't know what reputation the Seafarers' International Union has in that line but, all of a sudden, the gangsters disappeared.

SIU toughness worked just as well with communists in Canadian labour, Jodoin said: "The vipers have a way of sliding in sometimes where we don't want them, where they are not necessary and are not welcome. They had to go—we knew they had to go—and this has been accomplished."

Amidst the public celebration of his victory, it seemed impossible that anyone would challenge Banks' position as head of the Canadian SIU. Yet someone did. Not a high-ranking officer, but an ordinary sailor by the name of R.F. Lewis.

Everyone acknowledged that the CSU had been crushed. Why, then, was Banks still around? He was brought to Canada on a short-term basis to do a job, and now that job was done. Wasn't it time to give the Canadian District of the SIU the same autonomy enjoyed by all the union's other districts so that it could be democratically run by Canadians, not an unelected American appointee? Lewis thought so, and submitted the following resolution to the convention:

> WHEREAS the Canadian District of the Seafarers' International Union of North America requested the International Executive to take over this district and take whatever steps necessary to consolidate our position in the trade union movement, and
>
> WHEREAS the International Executive sent Brother Hal C. Banks to Canada in the position of Canadian District Administrator, and
>
> WHEREAS Brother Hal C. Banks so capably administered this District that we have taken over and signed contracts with the majority of vessels under Canadian registry, and
>
> WHEREAS in his "state of the union" report to this 1951 convention Brother Hal Banks stated that we are now in the position where we should be able to take over the jobs under our jurisdiction, and
>
> WHEREAS Brother Banks further stated that the Canadian District is now on its feet,
>
> THEREFORE BE IT RESOLVED that this convention go on record to apply to the International Executive at the next convention for the return of autonomy for this district.

Leonard ''Red'' McLaughlin, then in the process of becoming Banks' chief lieutenant, was having none of it. The angular, cerebral New Zealander—whom a B.C. judge would later describe as ''devious'' and ''unscrupulous,'' as well as ''clever, resourceful, and entirely untruthful''—argued against the resolution in a speech that appealed to the anti-communist hysteria of the times. It was also a good career move for McLaughlin, if only because it appealed to Banks' considerable ego:

> At the time this organization called the international for assistance, it was the culmination of a series of misfortunes, blunders and tragic events that had left the district without funds, without morale, and with only a handful of coastal vessels and one cable ship under contract, a section of the office staff was so corrupt and had no comprehension of the organizational opportunities which were still open to them in Canada. The district itself existed on the very brink of oblivion.
>
> Since that time, and due mainly to the efforts of the international representative, Mr. Hal C. Banks, we have made great strides in the acquisition of new contracts and better wages than have ever before been enjoyed by the Canadian seamen. We have more jobs and due to a sensible policy of full book issuance, a member is assured of job security to a point hitherto unthought of.
>
> However, apart from the international representative, we lack the dynamic leadership which is necessary to continue this pleasant state of affairs, and advance upon the opportunities of the yet untouched unorganized vessels under the Canadian flag. We do not possess enough men of experience in the negotiating field to continue the fight for wages and conditions. This fight demands the utmost in the forceful presentation of facts and demands. It calls for the finer subtleness of negotiating abilities.
>
> Therefore the man who is holding our negotiating and organizational program together is Mr. Hal C. Banks.
>
> The communists in our field are still lying dormant, and are eagerly awaiting the day when they can once again,

> through the democracy of our constitution, infiltrate into our ships, and set them up as hotbeds of dissension and sabotage. Some are within our ships already. They present a menace greater than that which is presented by the ship-owners. The international situation is the gravest it has yet been, through the treachery of the Kremlin in Korea. There is a frantic movement throughout the whole trade union movement to find and root out these traitors. . . .
>
> Autonomy is a fine thing, it is a true democracy and when it is assumed by a body it must be willing to accept its responsibilities as well as its advantages, and there is a question in my mind as to whether we are able, at this time, to accept the responsibility, whether we have the necessary leadership and everything that goes with it to take over the responsibilities of the autonomy.
>
> I think Mr. Banks—he is an international man, he is not a Seafarers' International Union Canadian District man, and my whole objection to the idea is that if we have to trade in Mr. Banks for autonomy, we can get along without the autonomy and that was the reason I objected to it.

Despite McLaughlin's attempts to sink it, the Lewis motion was carried. But Hal Banks was far from ousted. It would be three years before the Canadian District had any form of autonomy, and even then Banks wouldn't have to run for election. Elected officers would be entirely under his control. And he would take any steps necessary to make sure things stayed that way.

8

We got rid of that bastard.

Hal Banks describes how he silenced a Seafarers' dissident

Hal Banks had little tolerance for dissent, either real or perceived. But he had a particularly effective weapon against it in the Do Not Ship list. Essentially, it allowed Banks to prevent any union member from earning a living.

One such victim was dour, honest Jimmy Todd. Ironically, he had supported the move to bring Banks north to fight the CSU. He had even supported the temporary suspension of the union's constitution. And when other sailors complained about their lost rights, Todd argued that it was only temporary. Two years later there was no democracy and Todd was banned from sailing.

Banks refused to tell Todd why he had been blacklisted. There hadn't been any trial. There hadn't even been charges. However, there were rumblings that Banks suspected Todd of leading a protest strike against him. Todd tried to discuss his suspension but Banks refused to see him. The doorman at the Montreal hall wouldn't even let him in the building.

Todd believed in going through proper channels. With his kind eyes, slender build and receding hairline, he looked more like a high school science teacher than a waterfront reformer. If Banks was misusing his power, he would simply expose this to Banks' superiors and things would be set right. Todd and sailor Jack Brydson drew up a list of 3,000 sailors who had been labelled "commies, perverts, winos or epileptics" by Banks and blacklisted.

They took the list down to SIU headquarters in New York and presented it to vice-president Paul Hall. A brilliant man with almost no formal education, Hall was nicknamed "the Alabama

Alligator.'' His was a world of expediency, not theory. But he seemed sympathetic to Todd and Brydson, and they returned home to Canada optimistic about the chances of reform.

Not all the SIU dissidents in the Montreal district were so orderly. One blacklisted sailor borrowed a set of keys to the union hall from a fired employee and had them copied. He entered the hall early one morning and went on a rampage, destroying records and files and generally wrecking the hall. Then he made his way up to Banks' private office. He stole a photograph of Banks dressed in academic gowns and another where Banks was playing the ukelele. (They later appeared with sarcastic cutlines in a dissident newsletter, published by another blacklisted sailor.) Then, as an ultimate act of defiance, the protester dropped his pants and left a crude souvenir of his visit.

The next morning Banks was livid. Everyone involved in the cleanup was forbidden to speak about it. Banks liked to be seen as having total control. It wouldn't do for New York or San Francisco to know that someone had defecated on his plush office carpet.

But earnest Jimmy Todd believed in orderly protest. He and Brydson drafted a petition to the SIU North American executive which called for:

1. The immediate dismissal of Hal C. Banks as Director of the Canadian District of the Seafarers' International Union of North America.
2. Appointment of a member of the Canadian District as temporary Director acting in conjunction with an advisor appointed by the International Executive until such time as a convention can be called in the Canadian District wherein elections can be conducted in a Democratic manner.
3. A complete audit of the Canadian District books by a certified accountant appointed by the International Executive or by the new Canadian Director and Advisor.
4. Immediate revision of the ''Do Not Ship'' list as prescribed in the Constitution of the Seafarers' International Union of North America.

Todd, Brydson and former union newspaper editor Michael Davey signed the petition. They boasted of having four hundred signatures from Montreal alone, with more names arriving daily.

On September 15, Todd appealed directly to Harry Lundeberg for a trial so that he could fight his blacklisting. Two weeks later, he received a telegram from Hall and Morris Weisberger of the SIU executive board notifying him that his ''trial'' would be the next day. Hall and Weisberger had been in Montreal for some days meeting with Banks, but had only now informed Todd of the trial date. Banks received similar notification from Hall and Weisberger on the same date—although, as it turned out, this was mostly for appearance's sake.

When the interrogation started, it didn't take Todd long to realize that he was on trial, not Hal Banks. Blacklisted sailors who arrived to testify on Todd's behalf were stopped at the door and refused entry. There were officials from other unions present, but it was clear that they had no idea what was going on, as Todd was bullied, patronized and browbeaten by Hall. Banks sat back and enjoyed the show as Todd became flustered by Hall's line of questioning. To those reporters present, the distinct impression was given that Jimmy Todd, not Hal Banks, was to blame for the Do Not Ship list.

Hall grilled Todd about a news report stating that between two and four thousand sailors had been blacklisted. Hall wanted to know how many of these men were ''permit''—or probationary—members and how many were ''book''—or full—members:

> HALL: Are you aware of what the general rights and privileges of the permit men are in any particular group of the district? Are they entitled to any rights or privileges which normally belong to book men, Jimmy?
>
> TODD: They can attend meetings and have a voice, but no vote.
>
> HALL: They are, in fact, no more members of the Union than a cab driver on the street. Are they members or are they not?
>
> TODD: No.

Hall's curious comparison between dues-paying probationary members and cab drivers was a damning indictment of the union's membership structure. But all eyes were on Jimmy Todd, not Paul Hall or Hal Banks. And as the meeting dragged into the early hours of the morning, Todd knew he had lost. In an effort to salvage something from the whole disaster he decided not to release his petition against Banks, for fear that those who signed it would be "DNSed" as well.

Officially, sailors were promised fair trials, but no more was heard of Todd's case once the reporters had left. Hall said Todd could appeal his case before the union's international convention in 1953 in San Diego. Banks would even pay his way. Of course, both Hall and Banks knew that that would mean at least six more months before Todd could get back to work. And there was no way he could afford to bring witnesses to California. Besides, Todd realized, another trial would only mean another kangaroo court. Hall and Banks would again control the agenda and Hall had left no doubt his sympathies were with Banks.

"I am of the absolute opinion that you did make false accusations against Banks," Hall chastised. And he added, there were grounds for laying charges against Todd. But Hall said he wouldn't follow through with such charges, since "the record is mussed up enough now and is confusing enough as it is now."

Todd decided to withdraw his charges rather than turn in his petition. He had lost his case, but proved an important point: if the Canadian SIU was going to be reformed, it wouldn't be from the inside.

The dissident newsletter in which the stolen photos of Banks—in his academic regalia and ukelele-strumming pose—appeared was published by a blacklisted sailor who undertook the perilous task of repeatedly trying to unseat the waterfront warlord. His name was John Droeger.

Like Jimmy Todd, Droeger was never told why he had been blacklisted. He suspected it was because he had pointed out that there were insects in the crew's food during a voyage. Things got worse when the twenty-six-year-old sailor indicated at a

1952 meeting in Halifax that the union lacked a constitution, regular meetings, responsible accounting and a fair appeals process.

Droeger did not restrict himself to union channels, however, and he began to attack Banks where it hurt him the most—his image. In Ottawa, Opposition MPs were told about Banks' sordid criminal background, that he was an "alien gangster." Droeger went out of his way to help reporters expose union abuses. His private war became a full-time job when Banks' rival, Herbert McMaster of the United Mine Workers Mariners Division, hired him as a "union disorganizer." Droeger's job was to make life as miserable as possible for Banks.

There were others close to McMaster who simply wanted to murder Banks. A hardcore band of mine workers from Western Pennsylvania suggested killing Banks instead of just taunting him. But Droeger told them: "I don't want anything to do with that."

While he didn't want to end Banks' life, he had no qualms about making it miserable. Droeger and his friend Byron Ryan locked the outside doors of the Montreal SIU union hall with a chain and padlock during a meeting, then tipped off the press that a disturbance was taking place at Banks' headquarters. Eventually, one of Banks' men had to climb out of the building on a fire escape to cut the chain and free the union members who had crowded the hall.

When Droeger heard that Banks was heading to Switzerland for a convention, he cancelled reservations at two airlines, only to learn that Banks had reserved three separate sets of tickets. While Banks was overseas, Droeger sent him a bogus telegram instructing him to return home immediately for a union emergency. It cost more than $800 in long-distance fees and a considerable amount of anxiety before Banks realized he had been duped.

Droeger was relentless in his pursuit of Banks. Travelling to Banks' Pointe Claire home, he stripped naked and swam out in choppy, cold Lac Saint Louis to cut Banks' speedboat adrift. He was sawing the mooring rope with a paring knife when the lights in Banks' house were turned on suddenly. Droeger dived underwater to avoid being seen, smashing his head on the bottom in the process. When he poked his head out of the water and realized that Banks had just turned on the lights by coincidence, he finished cutting the rope. Banks' prized speedboat, with its custom Cadillac engine, drifted away and scraped noisily onto the nearby rocks. Even after he towelled off, Droeger had to sit on his hands to stop from shaking with cold and fear.

On several occasions, Droeger and Ryan would sit on the banks of the Lachine Canal and toss vitriolic anti-Banks propaganda onto passing ships. Their newsletter editorials constantly reminded SIU members of their boss's lavish spending habits.

A newspaper ad penned by Droeger read, "1954 Cadillac convertible. Bullet-proof construction . . . Reasons for selling . . . owner must leave country at once." At the bottom of the ad, Droeger listed Banks' home address as the place for prospective buyers to apply.

Banks had his phone number changed after receiving harassing calls. Undaunted, Droeger called Pointe Claire directory information and asked for the new number. He could hear a supervisor tell the operator what the new number was, but she explained that it was unlisted. Droeger jotted down the new number and called. Banks let out animal-like scream, then the line went dead. The next day Droeger learned that Banks had ripped his phone out from the wall.

Droeger's tactics hit their mark. Banks had a compulsion for control and Droeger was making a joke of him. As one rival union official recalls, "It was driving Banks around the bend." Soon the word was out that Banks was going to have Droeger killed. Droeger spent the summer of 1953 in navigation school in Britain. When he returned, people on the waterfront acted as if they had seen a ghost.

"We heard you were killed in England," they'd tell him.

"Well, I guess Hal wishes it, but it didn't happen," Droeger would say, laughing.

The final blow came when Droeger took Banks to court in 1954 to challenge the Do Not Ship list, which Banks had been using to generate funds by throwing out veteran members who were wise to his schemes and replacing them with new members, who had to pay hefty initiation fees. A Superior Court judge ruled in Droeger's favour and he signed aboard the *Canadian Constructor* as a reinstated member of the Seafarers' International Union.

In late 1954, Droeger took a short haul down the east coast. When they docked at Halifax, the ship's carpenter told him, "You know, you were not supposed to come back from this trip. I was supposed to kill you."

"What!"

"I don't know why I was supposed to do it. I don't do that sort of thing."

With that, the carpenter signed off the ship and Droeger took his job. On February 1, 1955, the *Constructor* sailed out of Montreal. It was the last time people in Montreal waterfront can recall seeing John Droeger.

The *Constructor* was to drop off a cargo in Philadelphia, then head to the West Indies. When the ship docked in Philadelphia, men claiming to be with FBI boarded and escorted Droeger off, saying he was believed to be a draft dodger. When he did not return, the word was that he had been murdered by men who had posed as FBI agents, and that Banks had been the man behind the *Constructor*'s detour to Philadelphia. Banks had set up a bogus trading company in Philadelphia, which in reality consisted only of a phone in a rented office. Then he paid between thirty and forty thousand dollars to ship one thousand tons of rubble to that phony trading company. The order was the minimum necessary to bring the *Constructor* to the eastern coast of the U.S., where Banks' associates included "Tough Tony" Anastasia of the International Longshoremen's Association, brother of contract-killer-turned-mob-boss Albert Anastasia. Such associations gave credibility to his boast that he could get rid of anybody. And according to Michael Sheehan, a Banks lieutenant throughout the 1950s, Banks bragged specifically about his role in Droeger's disappearance. Banks told him, "We got rid of that bastard."

Of course, Banks fanned the rumours that he had murdered Droeger. They were an effective means of showing the extent of his muscle. If he couldn't control Droeger in life, then he'd control his death. Nobody was laughing now.

9

John, be careful. You're dealing with some real bad people.

Liberal Labour Minister Milton Gregg's warning to John Droeger about the Seafarers' International Union

Harsh critics, and there would be many, would charge that Ottawa had a special set of rules for Hal C. Banks. More charitable commentators countered that the federal government was simply sloppy, dim-witted and generous to a fault.

Banks entered Canada in 1949 as a non-immigrant and was allowed to stay through a series of six-month extensions to his visa. But on May 8, 1952, Banks applied to become "landed," which gave notice of his intention to become a citizen. If his application was accepted, he could apply for citizenship in five years.

At that time, no one convicted of a crime was eligible for citizenship. Clearly this presented a problem for Banks, since he had been before a judge more often than some practising lawyers. At least, it should have. But when Banks filled out his application, the question "Have you ever been convicted of a criminal offense?" was mysteriously absent from his form. Banks didn't have to lie. The form did it for him. And although the government claimed that the omission was a typographical error made by the Queen's Printer, when *Toronto Star* reporter, Robert Reguly, tried to track down the errant forms, he was told that every one of them had been destroyed. Banks never did have to fill out a new, corrected application.

One wonders how Ottawa could not have known in 1952 of Banks' U.S. police record. It was common knowledge on the waterfront, and the Hammer murder trial of 1937 received broad coverage in major California newspapers, including *The Los Angeles Times*.

Only a few months after arriving in Montreal, Banks was up for possession of a sawed-off shotgun. He beat the charge, however, explaining: "The Commies went out and told the police that I went around armed to the teeth. Their lawyer swore out a warrant for me. But they couldn't prove anything. Heck, you can swear out a warrant against anybody for anything! Proving it is something else."

But it was proven in April 1952—a month before his application for landed status—that Banks had 36,000 smuggled cigarettes in his home. It wasn't the worst thing Banks could or would do, but it was a crime under the Customs Act none the less, and he was fined $200. As Banks explained it, however, he was a victim, a gracious host taken advantage of by an ungrateful guest. And somehow smuggling cigarettes was a very Canadian thing to do.

"A fellow came to my house with the cigarettes and offered them for sale," Banks said. "I bought them. That was a mistake. They weren't for resale. I planned to smoke some and give the rest away. I was framed in this deal. A 'friend' of mine who drank my liquor in my home and smoked my cigarettes, tipped off the RCMP. They came at 2 a.m. and asked, 'Do you have a supply of American cigarettes here?' I said it looked as if they were tipped off so they might as well go and get them. They went down to the exact corner of the basement where I kept them.

"I'm not saying it's right but everyone smokes smuggled cigarettes. I was in a lawyer's office the next day and he says, 'You must be short of smokes now so take some of mine,' and he offers me a few packs of smuggled smokes. Later that day, I noticed that a member of the RCMP had a half-smoked pack of American cigarettes on his desk. And out in the corridor of the same building everybody was smoking the same."

In January 1954, there was another weapons charge. Byron Ryan, a friend of Banks' critic John Droeger, had claimed that Banks pulled a pistol on him. It was very similar to his 1949 shotgun charge. And once again, the charges were dismissed.

According to Banks, "It was a false charge. He never even showed up in court. This fellow claims I drove up in my car and pointed a gun at him as he was walking along the street. Why I've never had a gun in my automobile in my life! Ryan couldn't have been very frightened of me. It took him a few months to make out the warrant against me."

Certainly Ryan hadn't intended to miss his court date. But the time of the trial was suddenly switched and he wasn't told of the change. Banks would brag that the last-minute change was brought about because he aimed dollars in the right direction. It didn't help appearances that he was reported joking with the trial judge in his office. "The patch was in," sailors would say of the switch.

Before his disappearance, John Droeger had attempted to focus the government's attention on Banks' activities. So when Labour Minister Milton Gregg announced that Banks would be one of Canada's representatives at an International Labour Organization (ILO) convention in Geneva, Droeger called Gregg's office to tell him that Banks was an alien and a gangster—two reasons why he wasn't a good representative for Canadian labour. Gregg listened politely and said he would get back to Droeger.

The next time they spoke, Gregg explained that the government had asked labour groups for names of people to nominate, then simply carried through with the nominations. Of course, Gregg continued, had the government known about Banks, "we never would have gone along with it. But it's too late now." Droeger then explained that he'd be passing on his information about Banks' background to the Opposition. Gregg said he understood, then added, "John, be careful. You're dealing with real bad people." His comments were about Banks, not the Opposition.

Droeger passed on his information to George Drew, Leader of the Opposition, and Ellen Fairclough (member for Hamilton West). They grilled the St. Laurent government over the wisdom of its decision to allow Banks to represent Canadian labour abroad. It was too late to have the trip cancelled, but the damage they did was real. The association with Banks was embarrassing for the Liberals.

The topic of Banks was discussed by Cabinet on February 25, 1954. Gregg explained again that although Banks was a Canadian representative at the ILO, he was representing labour and not Canada. Citizenship Minister Walter Harris added that Banks' court record hadn't been known when he was granted landed-immigrant status in 1952. Harris said a board of inquiry into Banks' case had been considered, with the possibility of deporting him. Now, with all the attention on Banks because of the ILO convention, perhaps it would be desirable to have a special inquiry officer study the case.

A special one-man inquiry was set up to examine Banks' status in Canada. While his only Canadian conviction was on the cigarette-smuggling charge, commissioner Jean St. Onge had the benefit of studying Banks' American record in a report that the RCMP had prepared on him in May 1953, and decided that where there was smoke there was fire. He recommended that Banks be deported for "moral turpitude." In his ruling St. Onge noted: "In view of the circumstances surrounding this case, and although the offences which he was charged with but was acquitted cannot naturally be considered as evidence, these charges nevertheless reveal this person to be rather ruthless in his methods. It is my opinion that he will undoubtedly run afoul of our laws and I would recommend dismissal of his appeal."

Banks' appeal was quickly dismissed. A letter was drawn up for Immigration Minister Walter Harris to make the expulsion official:

> In the matter of the Appeal of Harold Chamberlain BANKS, also known as Hal C. BANKS, pursuant to the provisions of the Immigration Act, ordered deported at Montreal, P.Q. on the 29th June, 1954;
>
> WHEREAS I have considered the proceedings of the Inquiry and the evidence and testimony presented therein; and
>
> WHEREAS I have examined all the circumstances of this appeal;
>
> WHEREFORE, I do dismiss the said appeal.

When the form came to Harris, he made just one change. He stroked out the word "dismiss," substituted "allow," and signed it. It was his last day in office and left his successor Jack Pickersgill one less problem to deal with. Two days later, the director of immigration put a better face on things. He ruled that a conviction under the Customs Act like Banks' cigarette offence didn't connote a crime involving moral turpitude, even though a crime under the Excise Act did. This contradicted advice given to the Immigration Department by the Ministry of Justice in December 1952 regarding Banks' citizenship case.

Nevertheless, the cleansing by the Liberals was to be made complete. An order-in-council was passed granting him landed immigrant status, stating he "appears to have been successfully rehabilitated." Now he could be deported only for treason, spying, sabotage, drug possession or subversion.

Exactly what happened during the flurry of activity that led to Banks' landed-immigrant status remains fuzzy. A disaffected Banks lieutenant would tell Harry Crowe, of the Canadian Brotherhood of Railway, Transport and General Workers (CBRT), that money changed hands somewhere along the line. Crowe heard of a frantic rush to Ottawa on June 29, 1954. In the SIU car was a union official, an immigration department official, and a Montreal lawyer with a terrible drinking problem and excellent Liberal connections. They brought with them two envelopes. Crowe's informant believed that one of them contained cash.

When the men reached Ottawa, they checked into the Lord Elgin Hotel, where they picked up a clean shirt for the lawyer's appearance and a bottle of whisky for his spirits. They dined at La Touraine restaurant with two MPs and the lawyer's sister, the secretary of a Cabinet minister, while the immigration man checked into his offices. Late that night, the lawyer and his sister headed for Parliament Hill.

When he returned to the Lord Elgin, the lawyer, whose father had been a Montreal organizer for the Liberals, was beaming. "I've got it fixed," he announced. "Banks has got his citizenship."

Banks was overjoyed when he was told over the phone of the news. The lawyer, who was later disbarred, was set up in an apartment on Dorchester Street and given SIU legal work.

Full details of what happened that day may lie in those Immigration and RCMP files that still remain closed to the public. Of fifty-seven files at the Department of Immigration concerning Banks' 1954 deportation inquiry, only six can be obtained through the Access to Information Act. Of the six open files, one is a photocopy from Hansard available at any public library and another is Banks' appeal form, which reporter Robert Reguly provided for *Toronto Star* readers more than two decades ago. Employment and Immigration Canada claims that the material is either too private, was obtained during a police investigation or might "reasonably be expected to be injurious to the enforcement of any law in Canada."

More than twenty years after making the decision that allowed Banks to stay in Canada, Walter Harris still believes his judgement was correct. "What we had to consider was one actual conviction in the U.S.A. and the cigarette charge. As against this, we had to consider his record of breaking the hold of the Communist Party on the union and also the fact that he had been in the country for—what?—five years, and had landed status for two years. . . . I don't remember any record of internal fighting other than the business with the communists. . . . From the end of the war until ten or twelve years later, the relationship with Russia was not good and there was a genuine fear on all sides of the consequences."

The problem, of course, was that Hal Banks got to decide who the communists were. In the absence of any clear definition, a communist became anyone who disagreed with Hal Banks.

In Banks' favour, Harris remembers taking into consideration reports that Banks had married a Canadian woman after arriving in Montreal. The reports were true, but then so were the stories that she had left him after suffering repeated beatings. Shortly after returning from the ILO convention in Geneva, the new Mrs. Banks was spotted fleeing from Banks' Cadillac on a busy Montreal street to escape another attack.

For all of Banks' appearances in court, Harris noted that his only major U.S. conviction was the cheque charge that put him in San Quentin, a record subsequently erased by California Governor Earl Warren.

Harris today bristles at suggestions that there was anything improper in his decision. He urges a study of his briefing papers, but an application to obtain them under the Access to Information Act was refused. He notes it isn't uncommon for men to brag of having influence in Ottawa which in fact doesn't exist. Of reports that he attended some of Banks' parties in Montreal,

Harris said, "I never did. I was at no party or entertainment of any kind with him at any time."

Jack Pickersgill, advisor to both Mackenzie King and Louis St. Laurent, and a key Ottawa insider at the time Banks was brought to Canada, says that he had never heard of Banks until June 30 or July 1, 1954, when he took over from Harris: "I can't say positively. I wouldn't take an oath that I might not have read something in the newspapers but I don't remember it. I didn't know anything about the fellow. You know, I had other things to do."

In fact, Pickersgill's name appears in the minutes of a February 25, 1954, session of Cabinet in which Banks was a major topic of discussion. Told of this evidence, Pickersgill acknowledges the possibility.

"I was at the meeting, I think, but I don't have any remembrance of it. You see, I wasn't the Minister of Immigration at that time. I was the Secretary of State and I was the House Leader, and I had a lot of other considerations that mattered a lot more to me than anything about Banks. . . . It's not absolutely certain I was at the meeting when the discussion took place but I probably was. But it obviously made no real impression on me."

Both Harris' and Pickersgill's memories of Banks' 1937 murder trial vary greatly from the actual Hammer case. Newspaper accounts of the day reported that Hammer was beaten to death in a barroom brawl, started because it infuriated Banks to hear a white man speaking Spanish to a barmaid. But according to Harris and Pickersgill the circumstances were something far different. It took place at a snack bar, not a beverage room. And instead of Banks picking on a bar patron, Harris and Pickersgill say Banks was harassed by three union foes while returning home from work. Harris had heard that Banks tried to lock himself in his car, but that the three men dragged him out. While defending himself, Banks knocked one of the men down and he struck his head on a stone curb. The fall was enough to kill the man, Harris recounts.

Because of the Immigration Department's refusal to release Harris' briefing papers, unsettling questions linger. Did Banks kill at least two men in California? Was Harris improperly briefed? How could Pickersgill not have heard of Banks five years after he was brought to Canada? Pickersgill was a central political figure in Ottawa and Banks had anything but a low profile. The views of Harris and Pickersgill on Banks are all the more curious in that they differ so sharply from the opinion of their former Cabinet colleague Milton Gregg, who described Banks and his cronies as "some real bad people."

Even super-Liberal Pickersgill admits things might have been handled better:

> It seems to me there are two things it's quite reasonable to criticize the Liberal government for. One is [for] encouraging the shipping companies to get this fellow in to replace the Seamen's Union with the Seafarers' International Union. But the extenuating circumstances were certainly very considerable because there was an obvious, serious disruption of shipping at that time and I don't suppose that anyone in the government really knew very much about this Seafarers' International Union. Certainly, [we] wouldn't have known very much about Banks, because he seems mostly to have established his reputation after he came to Canada. But I think that it's a subject of reasonable criticism.
>
> And I think it's also a subject of reasonable criticism that not enough seems to have been known about him when he was sent to Geneva, and it would have been so easy for the government to have objected on the ground that he wasn't a Canadian citizen and said to the Trades and Labour Congress, "Surely there must be some Canadian you could send." But I think those are both grounds for criticism. I don't agree on either case that it was necessarily a very grave thing, but I do think you can reasonably criticize.
>
> But once he had been here . . . whatever else you may say, we had no strikes.

10

Now I can go places.

Hal Banks, January 1957

On January 28, 1957, Harry Lundeberg died of a heart attack at the age of fifty-six. He had been admitted to hospital for what was thought to be a mild heart attack and was expected to be released within days. The entire sailing fraternity was shocked, and none more so than Hal Banks. As SIU vice-president Ed Turner remembers, Lundeberg's death was probably the worst event in Banks' life. At the San Francisco funeral, "He was just standing there shaking. I don't say he was crying, he was just shaking. . . . You could see convulsions. . . . I didn't see him actually crying. But he was physically shaken up. I don't think Banks was the same guy after that."

Perhaps Lundeberg filled a void left by the poor relationship Banks had had with his father. Perhaps Banks envied the emotional hold Lundeberg had over his men. Perhaps he was genuinely grateful that Lundeberg had given him power. Whatever the reasons, Banks' respect for Lundeberg was genuine.

Ed Turner remembers that Lundeberg was "the only guy that Hal Banks ever trusted . . . ever levelled with." This is certainly true. Lundeberg knew Banks' strengths, weaknesses and what buttons to push to make him do things. When Lundeberg would hear that Banks was drunk with his new-found power, he would slap him back into line with a phone call.

"You're playing big shot up there," Lundeberg would say. "Now goddamn it, knock it off!"

And, for a time, Banks would settle down. Federal politicians, shippers and right-wing unionists who had backed Banks in 1949 saw Lundeberg as a safety valve. If Banks was a trained attack dog, Lundeberg was his handler.

"I think it was Harry Lundeberg's power and strength that kept the union operating as a union," recalls former Banks lieutenant Michael Sheehan. "To my estimation, that [Lundeberg's death] was the end of the SIU as a democratic union."

Banks dug deep into the Montreal district SIU coffers and donated $25,000 to ensure Lundeberg's children would be educated. But it wouldn't be long until he started digging deeper into union funds, for himself. A better man might have decided this was the time to put Lundeberg's philosophies into action and become an honest unionist. The battle with the CSU was long since over and the shippers were quiescent, so maintaining peace wouldn't have been difficult.

While Banks felt the emotional loss of Lundeberg, instinctively he saw an opening. No longer would he get calls from San Francisco telling him to smarten up. Power was a narcotic for Banks and Lundeberg's death made him a more powerful man. As the heads of fiefdoms within the SIU jostled for power in the new post-Lundeberg order, suddenly he was a force to be reckoned with.

Michael Sheehan was at a meeting with Banks and second-in-command Red McLaughlin in January 1957, shortly after Lundeberg's death. Banks was talking about what a great man Lundeberg had been and how much he would be missed. But then the conversation changed dramatically.

"Well, now I can go places," Banks said. "Well, I am going to make a motion that I raise my salary from $12,000 to $20,000 a year," whereupon he stood up and said, "I second the motion." Then he sat back down again before his huge desk, saying, "Accepted."

From now on, Hal Banks was going to have things his way. Nothing—or nobody—was going to interfere.

Captain Henry Walsh sensed something was a little strange when he drove into the parking lot of his hotel in Owen Sound, Ontario, on August 18, 1957. The lot was usually lit at 11:15 at night, but now it was dark. Like most people who dared to oppose Hal Banks publicly, Walsh had a tendency to notice anything out of the ordinary.

The previous week, Walsh, an organizer and business agent with the Canadian Merchant Service Guild—whose membership drew from ship's officers—had called Banks a goon, a thug and a coward in front of the crew of a vessel docked at Montreal. Of course, Walsh had been saying those things for years. He had even said them to Banks' face. But he was a little more on guard than usual while on this organizing trip—particularly as he had heard that a carload of Banks' goons had arrived in Owen Sound.

Just to be safe, Walsh took another turn around the block before heading into the lot, which appeared empty. But when he went to take his suitcase out of the trunk, he heard someone in the darkness call his name. It was an unfamiliar voice, but he answered it as if by reflex. Suddenly the trunk door was slammed down on him. He would later wonder if the first fist that struck him was holding a blackjack or a club. Through the kicks, punches, pain and numbness that followed, he heard the unfamiliar voice say: "This will keep you off the waterfront."

"Let's shoot him," someone suggested.

"No, you can't do that. We're not supposed to shoot him," another stranger replied.

Stunned and unable to see through the dark and the pain, Walsh couldn't tell how many men were beating him, except that the kicks came too quickly for just one attacker. He kept thinking he had to get back on his feet or be beaten to death. He had no idea of how long he fought to stand up, only recalling that he was repeatedly smashed back onto the pavement.

He tasted blood from having his teeth kicked out. Clothing and skin were ripped from his legs, back and arms. Finally, the beating subsided. Hovering on the brink of consciousness, Walsh pulled himself back into his hotel.

When the police arrived, they didn't seem too interested. Walsh didn't really expect them to be. He had learned it was futile to go to the police against Hal Banks. Perhaps they'd figure it was an Ottawa matter to be filed and forgotten. Or they might decide not to push it because witnesses against Hal Banks had a habit of reconsidering things and backing down. It didn't really matter this time anyway. Between the darkness of the parking lot and his semi-conscious condition, Walsh couldn't give a description of who had beaten him. He wasn't even sure how many attackers there were.

When the police left, Walsh staggered into his car, not knowing if he had any serious internal injuries or if he'd be conscious much longer. All he knew was that he wanted out of Owen Sound.

When he reached his Welland home 150 miles later, Walsh couldn't get inside his house without his wife Phyllis' aid. He remembered nothing of the drive. A couple of days later, someone from the SIU was at Walsh's door checking to see if Walsh had made it home.

Getting beaten up didn't come as a surprise for Henry Walsh. If anything, he was a little surprised it hadn't been worse. Walsh had openly defied Hal Banks and he knew that the consequences for this were severe. Moreover, he had defeated Banks repeatedly when he had gone to the Labour Relations Board following SIU raids on his members. And he was constantly on the waterfront telling the officers that it wasn't right for Hal Banks to take over their union.

But Hal Banks was determined to win. He called Walsh into his penthouse office and outlined his options: first, he could agree to sign over to Banks the 2,000 ship's officers in his union and be rewarded with a big office at the SIU hall in Montreal, a hefty salary and a non-existent workload. But Walsh refused. He wouldn't even talk money with Banks.

"You know, if you don't turn them in, there's other ways of getting them," Banks said.

"Well, you go ahead."

Then Banks described Walsh's second option: to have his legs broken, and then sign over the union. Walsh had already heard about Banks' "pavement treatment" in which the victim was thrown on the street so that his legs were raised up onto a curb and then a hired goon leapt onto them, snapping the bones like twigs. Banks would boast that Jack Casper was a master of the technique.

Walsh's third option was to simply disappear, at which time

Banks would take over the union. Walsh had heard how close Banks was to members of the mob in Montreal's East End, and knew it wasn't an idle threat. But Walsh wouldn't be intimidated. "Oh, you wouldn't do it," Walsh replied. "You wouldn't have enough guts to do it. You'd pay somebody to do it." This said, the five foot four, forty-six-year-old Walsh pulled himself up to his full height and marched out of the office. He knew Banks was furious.

Afterwards, Walsh stayed out of dark alleys. He avoided late-night calls to ships. When he checked them out, he usually found they were phony and just a ploy to draw him to the waterfront. He didn't drink but even if he had, he would have avoided bars. "That was death," he would say. "You could disappear from a bar so easily. . . ."

He was leery of strangers. Once when he was in Windsor for negotiations with a steamship company, a young woman showed up at his motel room moments after he returned for the night. She wanted to use his phone, she said, even though there was a phone nearby in the lobby. He sent her away, sure that she was trying to check if he was travelling alone. He remembered that the night before the Owen Sound beating, someone who appeared to be the same woman was standing by his hotel's entrance when he came in. The next morning, she followed him into a nearby coffee shop, then called someone from a pay phone. "I knew I had to watch everything," Walsh said.

It was obvious why Banks so desperately wanted the Canadian Merchant Service Guild. With the crews', the engineers' and the officers' unions, Banks would have total control of the Seaway. He'd then have the shipowners "right in the palm of his hands," Walsh says. "He could write his price. I think he had the idea he could be Prime Minister of Canada some day. I think he really thought that once he controlled all the shipping in Canada, then he could run the whole goddamn country."

Walsh had seen what happened to others who gave in to Banks, and he was determined it wouldn't happen to him. "I knew that if I had given in, I wouldn't be able to get a job anywhere," he recalls. "I spent my life in this business. I didn't want someone like Banks to take it away."

Walsh hadn't considered the old Canadian Seamen's Union so tough to deal with. He didn't buy the argument that Banks was an anti-communist crusader. Rather, he considered Banks a boorish American thug who had no business leading a union of ship's officers. Walsh had no illusions about winning single-handedly, but, "I was sticking in there mister. I was hanging in there and praying. I was determined that he'd have to do away with me."

The beating of Henry Walsh was ordered in Banks' penthouse office. Union regular Paul Karsh acted as the fingerman, and fled when the beating got too gruesome. Eldon Richardson was a utility thug who helped in the beating. Jack Casper, who rounded out the team, was something far different. He was already notorious for his fight with Banks at the Sailors' Union hall and, in fact, he had fought professionally. He had been a sparring partner of Buddy Baer back in the 1930s when Baer was world heavyweight champion. Though he never became a champion himself, he did develop a professional attitude towards beating men for pay. He could pummel someone with the detachment of an assembly-line worker; or, if the job inspired him, he could pound someone with a savagery that made him appear possessed. When Henry Walsh got in a few punches in the darkened Owen Sound parking lot, Richardson thought Casper was going to beat Walsh to death.

11

To handle seamen, it is a tough job. He has to be tough.

Frank Hall of the Brotherhood of Railway and Steamship Clerks on Hal Banks' methods

If some unions, such as Henry Walsh's Merchant Service Guild, were unwilling to play ball with Hal Banks, there were others who would. So one of Banks' next targets was the National Association of Marine Engineers (NAME), whose national president, Dick Greaves, was sitting in Banks' office when the order was given for the beating that almost killed Henry Walsh.

There was no doubt what Banks meant when he ordered big Jack Casper and his two helpers to "do a job" on Walsh. But Greaves didn't warn Walsh or tip off the police. He wasn't a hero, and while union men might not have respected him, at least he had his health. And if he played his cards right, he stood to gain by cozying up to Banks. Being respected and getting along with Hal Banks didn't seem to go together.

Banks had been playing a game of divide and conquer with NAME for several years. Originally, his attentions had been directed towards John McGough and John Stirling, of the union's Eastern and Great Lakes Division. In the mid-1950s, Banks told Stirling he fancied the idea of a merger between NAME and the SIU. Of course, it would be under the auspices of the Seafarers'—and Banks would be calling the shots. Banks suggested Stirling move into the SIU office to make the operation more tidy.

Stirling explained that NAME had a constitution and that, even if he wanted to, he couldn't take such a drastic step without a union meeting and vote.

Banks was appalled.

"That's no fucking way to run a union!" he exploded. "Don't give those fuckers democracy." He jabbed a finger at a picture of

Dave Beck, Teamster president and former retainer of goon Jack Casper. "That fucker knows how to run a meeting. I'll show you how to run a meeting."

With a flourish, Banks summoned in one of his executives and told him that he wanted $2,000 added onto his salary. This was to be drafted onto union minutes, he pronounced. Moments later, Banks was handed minutes stating he had been voted a $2,000 raise. He then told Stirling that he too could drive an Eldorado convertible and offered to pick up the tab, something Stirling could never do on his $225 monthly salary. Stirling refused the car and the offer to work for the SIU. Banks' demeanour changed abruptly. "Okay boys, I've been nice," he shouted. "Now I'm going to turn the heavy artillery on you."

Banks' strategy was to take advantage of a provision under Quebec law that allowed citizens to swear out arrest warrants. On Friday afternoons pairs of SIU workers were sent to swear out warrants against NAME officials. Their timing meant victims would be stuck in jail for the weekend. By the time the case was to come before a judge, the complainants would be aboard a freighter in a foreign port.

Stirling was dragged off to jail three times on totally groundless charges. When he didn't buckle, Banks broadened his attack. New victims included the NAME office secretary. A proper mother of two, she was forced to spend a night in a police holding tank with drunks and prostitutes.

Stirling's car was broken into and he lost a mass of union correspondence and files. They turned up in SIU offices, and Greaves heard SIU men brag about the theft. Banks also had the masthead for the NAME newspaper stolen, and printed an issue which damned McGough and Stirling as thieves.

Stirling regularly received threatening phone calls late at night until one night when he got a call from a man who said that all was forgiven. Hal had changed his mind and wanted nothing more than an end to the ugliness. Moments later there was another call. It was the same voice but this time it was snickering, "Hey, have you seen the colour of your car lately?" While Stirling had been handling the first call, someone had splashed a rainbow of paint on his car. On another occasion piano tuners showed up at the house when there was no piano to be tuned.

Then a man arrived with a truckload of coal and prepared to dump it on the driveway, although the house had no coal furnace.

Some pranks had a grimmer twist. ''Virtually every undertaker in St. Catharines was sent there to make arrangements,'' Stirling recalls, ''to pick up the body.''

Stirling almost did provide work for the undertaker. One night he was walking across a concrete bank of the Welland Canal when a man swinging a length of heavy chain approached him. Stirling turned and saw his retreat blocked by a man holding a heavy leather belt with a pronounced metal buckle. Before they could reach him, Stirling jumped what seemed to be a hundred feet onto the ground below, escaping his would-be attackers but winding up in hospital as a result of the leap.

Sometimes men would zip across his lawn in tiny Volkswagen ''bugs.'' By the time police could be called, the marauding Volkswagens would be long gone. It was the drivers who hurt Stirling the most. One of them crashed into his German shepherd, Susie, leaving her lying on the pavement with two broken hind legs. The dog lived, but she was never the same.

As Hal Banks was alternately wooing and intimidating rival unions that he wanted to bring into the SIU fold, he was applying to become a Canadian citizen. But there was a problem. Because of what he called ''a couple lousy cigarettes''—36,000 to be exact—that had been smuggled and ended up in his basement, he might lose his chance to become a Canadian.

If he wasn't a citizen, Banks aspirations to higher office would be thwarted. And now his enemies had even hired Pinkerton detectives to dredge up his criminal record. Was this any way to treat Canada's anti-communist crusader? He was, after all, the man who had stopped the Red tide from engulfing the waterfront.

To support his application in the spring of 1957, Banks brought Claude Jodoin, president of the newly formed Canadian Labour congress (CLC) into court as a character witness. The CLC had only come into being in 1956, with the amalgamation of the Canadian Congress of Labour and the Trades and Labour Congress of Canada. Jodoin was by nature a conciliator and believed good things would happen for his members through unity. Labour was moving into an era when it could take full part in the political life of Canada. In-fighting only hurt the cause and gave labour a bad name.

Jodoin, tall, handsome and eminently respectable, testified that Hal Banks was "un actif pour le Canada."

"You think that a man who has been before the Court about twelve times is recommendable?" asked lawyer William Miller, who was acting for John McGough, John Ellis and John Stirling of the National Association of Marine Engineers.

"It all depends on the nature of the charges," Jodoin replied.

There was a fair variety to choose from. Banks' three decades of crime had earned him court dates for murder, burglary, child stealing, assault causing bodily harm, possession of a sawed-off shotgun, intimidation and defamatory libel.

Montreal police captain Horace Thivierge saw nothing wrong with Banks' morality and told the court just that. Roger Provost, president of the Quebec Federation of Labour and vice-president of the Canadian Labour Congress, also lent his support, testifying that Banks had not only conducted himself well, but was also a sober fellow. Provost did qualify his comments, however, noting that he only knew Banks professionally, not personally. Next on the stand was Louis Laberge, who told the court of his great admiration for Banks. Laberge's comment carried the weight of his roles as business agent of the International Association of Machinists, executive member of the Montreal Labour Council and Montreal city councillor.

Frank Hall of the Brotherhood of Railway and Steamship Clerks, who helped bring Banks north in 1949, dismissed the cigarette-smuggling conviction as minor. Hall praised Banks for cleaning up a union which had been "infested with communists." Violence, it seemed, was a necessary evil. "To handle seamen, it is a tough job," Hall said. "He has to be tough."

Banks also threw the weight of church and civic groups behind him, since they hadn't done it themselves. In the world of Hal Banks, you were either for him or against him. And since the church and civic groups hadn't formally opposed him, Banks' lawyer John Ahern argued, they must be for him. To make this claim seem a little more credible, Ahern also tried to put to rest stories that Banks bragged of a close working relationship with East End hitmen.

"What do you have to say about getting rid of anybody in Montreal for $1,500, as alleged by Mr. John McGough, John G. Ellis and John Stirling?" Ahern asked.

"If I recall correctly, this was to retire certain officials," Banks replied. "Otherwise I deny their statements. They are not true."

Those opposing Banks were a considerably less distinguished bunch, as unemployed sailors tended to be. Blacklisted sailor Morris Marrinan had the courage to say Banks was "a noted bully and a most outstanding tyrant" who "has caused untold sufferings, hardships and misery to Canadian Flag Seamen." It was a misery that had clearly taken its toll on Marrinan. A former boxing champion in Ireland, he had become a pitiful sight since being blacklisted. His grip on reality was loose, his mind tortured; he was often seen wandering along University Street, his life possessions in a couple of shopping bags. He was a walking testament to what happened when you crossed Hal Banks.

Omer Boudreau and Byron Ryan, friends of the now-missing John Droeger, were there to call Banks a criminal. Sailor Richard Jurkiewicz told the court that he had to pay what was described as a "tribute" to work for the union from 1950 to 1955. Another eighteen sailors took their turns describing Banks' "terrorist" methods of controlling sailors, how he arbitrarily threw out longstanding union members, as well as how he bought personal property with union funds.

John Stirling and Jack McGough, the NAME officers he had courted when he thought he could seduce the marine engineers into SIU hands, related chilling stories of their time with Banks. Stirling described how Banks had sent him west to stir up trouble in labour circles. He produced a letter written by Banks, dated February 15, 1955:

Mr. Norman G. Cunningham,
Seafarers' International Union of North America,
298 Main Street,
Vancouver 4, B.C.

Dear Norm,

This will introduce Mr. J.M. Sterling [*sic*], the representative of the Government Seafarers' and Dockyard Workers' Union, our chartered affiliate. He is going to work on the Engineers and Mates on the West Coast, and we are helping them out at the present time. . . .

". . . We are going to try to give McKie and Bullock the business. We are tired of letting these cockroaches clutter up our kitchen. See what you can do, and let me know how things are going. . . ."

Herbert Mockeridge, president of the tiny Montreal Steel and Foundry Workers' Union, had also joined the fight against Banks. Blacklisted ex-SIU men had flocked to Mockeridge when he challenged Banks for dredges and tugs in the Montreal area. For his troubles, he had been harassed and called a thug in the *Canadian Sailor*. It was a curious insult, as "thug" Mockeridge stood at only five foot six and was slightly built. Mockeridge had also taken exception to a recent article about himself in the newspaper under the headline "A real bad stink." The editorial style was vintage *Canadian Sailor*: "When this worm was brought out from under his slimy rock, the stench was so bad . . . it was almost nauseating."

Banks stayed cool throughout the proceedings, never showing anything but respect to NAME lawyer William Miller. The same could not be said, however, of the telephone callers who harassed Miller throughout the night, or the men with the power tractor who tore up McGough's garden at 4:00 a.m. Ahern didn't share his client's unflappability. He had been a lawyer about as many years as Miller had been alive, and he shot Miller a look of disgust when the NAME counsel introduced Banks' criminal record. "Are you cuckoo or something by suggesting that a guy who has been before the courts is not entitled to Canadian citizenship?" Ahern asked. Miller, thirty-one and just four years out of law school, surprised himself with his reply. "Mr. Ahern," he shot back, "I think you are cuckoo if you're serious about suggesting that we ought to let in this kind of character as a citizen of this country."

Miller remembers that when he introduced Banks' record, he couldn't help feel like David when he saw Goliath toppling. "I remember it was a Friday and I had spent the entire day cross-examining Banks. And all of his gory background came out. I was waiting for the Saturday paper, which came out Friday night. I remember . . . picking up a *Gazette* and [seeing] some glorifying headline about Banks making [a] presentation and John Ahern showing what a glowing citizen he was to be if he was admitted. I couldn't believe it. I concluded right then and there that there had to be a payoff to make black look white and white look black. . . . It was really a remarkable mistreatment of the news, but that was an old story and we were aware of that."

Miller also knew that he'd have to be convincing before Citizenship Judge Paul Fontaine. All things being even—or even close to even—Banks would win. "Paul Fontaine was a very, very quiet, conservative-minded type of citizenship judge," Miller said. "I don't think when the hearing started that there was a chance in hell that they were going to refuse his request for citizenship."

But Fontaine listened to Miller and his associates. In his judgement on April 10, 1958, he commented that "the Applicant being now 49 years of age cannot be considered as a juvenile delinquent." He noted that Judge Frederick Collins had doubted Banks' truthfulness in the Droeger lawsuit back in 1954. Fontaine also saw that on four of Banks' acquittals, his co-accused were convicted or committed to trial.

Fontaine also wasn't too impressed by Banks' pardon, which Pickersgill and Harris had earlier cited as proof of rehabilitation. "The courts hearing citizenship applications, in the United States, are rather reluctant about pardons," Fontaine wrote, " . . . It is only natural that a Canadian Court hearing the application of an American citizen should display a similar prudence."

Banks' application for citizenship was dismissed. He could stay in Canada unless he was caught committing a major crime, but he could never hold public office. It was a crushing blow to him. He became paranoid about travelling outside Canada, as he was deathly afraid that the Diefenbaker government wouldn't let him back into the country. Ironically, a decade later, the day he had been refused citizenship would seem to be one of the luckiest days in Hal Banks' life.

12

Everything that floats is in our jurisdiction and everything that floats is going to be organized by us.

Hal Banks

When Hal Banks started backing Dick Greaves against the Eastern and Great Lakes District of NAME, he did so in the expectation that Greaves would walk the SIU line. And for a while, amidst increasingly bitter power struggles among the various NAME factions, Greaves obliged, often dropping by Banks' office for coffee and chummy conversation. The relationship did not last, however, and soon Banks had shifted his support to more pliable elements of the union.

By the summer of 1958, Banks' tangled relationship with NAME had reached new Machiavellian heights. The SIU was striking CPR ferries and Banks seemed to be making no effort whatsoever to settle.

NAME officials suspected Banks was trying to drive CPR ferries out of business—a strategy that would aid the plans of William Bennett's Social Credit government in British Columbia to set up its own ferry service. It would also endear Banks to Black Ball Ferries, Canadian Pacific's only competitor for the ferry service between Vancouver Island and the mainland. Those who knew Banks also knew that he was no stranger to a sweetheart deal. Fearing that this would cost their members jobs, the marine engineers called a legal strike against Black Ball to force the issue to a head.

Premier Bennett set up a meeting with the SIU, the Canadian Merchant Service Guild and NAME at the Hotel Vancouver. The marine engineers agreed to attend but did nothing more. Greaves refused even to speak to Attorney General Robert Bonner. Friday night, all day Saturday and Sunday morning passed with no negotiations. Greaves just sat there drinking coffee and waiting for the government to blink. "We didn't talk about anything," Greaves recalls. "Then on the Sunday afternoon they said to us, 'We've got reservations on the plane for you and you'll be in the premier's office tomorrow morning at ten o'clock.' So we went over. When we got there, we were ushered to Bennett's place and he just said to all of us, 'Will you cooperate with the government?' . . . When he came to me, I said, 'What do you mean cooperate, Mr. Premier?' He said, 'I'm asking the questions. Will you cooperate with this government?' I said, 'I can't cooperate until I know what cooperate means. What does it stand for?' He got mad as hell. He said, 'I'm asking the questions here and you had better cooperate.' " Bennett angrily ended the meeting, telling the union officials to return to his office at two that afternoon.

It was during his taxi ride back, just before two o'clock, that Greaves heard on the radio that the Civil Defence Act had been invoked. A few minutes later, Greaves says, a Cabinet minister read the proclamation to the labour men in person. "You can't do that," Greaves recalls himself saying. "You can't do that legally."

"I know that," the Cabinet minister replied. "I'll see you in the Supreme Court in five years time. In the meantime, get your people back to work or they'll all be under an injunction and in jail."

The marine engineers had made their point. Black Ball ferries were also ordered back to work. The engineers had also managed to focus B.C. labour criticism on Banks for what smelled of a sweetheart deal.

Banks' machinations had alienated not only NAME but also the Canadian Brotherhood of Rail and Transport Workers (CBRT). With its 40,000 members, the CBRT was almost four times larger than the SIU and, as Banks would soon discover, it was an enemy he could ill afford.

The SIU's dispute with the CBRT had its seeds in the building of the Canso causeway. The link between Cape Breton Island and Nova Scotia in 1955 spelled the end of the ferry service between the island and mainland. CNR employees belonging to CBRT, some with as many as forty years of experience, were now faced with the loss of their jobs and little hope of finding something new. When CBRT president Bill Smith learned that a new ferry service was being developed by CNR between Yarmouth and Bar Harbor, Maine, he approached CNR president Donald Gordon, in the hope that the laid-off ferry workers could find work on the new ship, the M.V. *Bluenose*. Since the *Bluenose* was a much larger vessel than the old ferry, there would be a need for additional employees to man it. Smith found Gordon agreeable. "It was not a signed agreement. It was just a general understanding that these people would be given the first opportunity of employment."

Delays in building the *Bluenose* meant that it was ready for its sea trial just as the St. Lawrence was beginning to ice up in the fall of 1955. The builders had scrambled to get the ship out into the Gulf or the Atlantic before it was too late. "There was a mad dash to get the ship out of the shipyard and out into the St. Lawrence," Smith recalls. "They called SIU . . . for a skeleton crew to get the ship out. . . . The shipbuilding company had no knowledge of the . . . agreement that I had with Mr. Gordon."

When the ship was turned over to the CNR, Banks immediately claimed that it was an SIU ship, since his union members had manned it for its sea trial.

Canadian Labour Congress president Claude Jodoin was called in to mediate during a meeting at the Mount Royal Hotel in Montreal. Smith was adamant that his members be given first rights to the available jobs. "He felt that I had a moral obligation to his people to find them employment, and particularly in the service of the CNR because the pension, their vacations, seniority and all of the other rights that they had accumulated over many long years were at stake."

Banks blustered that this was irrelevant. He manned it for the sea trial. It was his ship.

The meeting dragged on throughout the afternoon with no movement on either side. Jodoin sat in the middle, patiently trying to find some middle ground. Finally, Smith lost patience. Surely Banks must agree that the laid-off employees had a right to work on the *Bluenose*. ''Nope,'' Banks replied. ''Everything that floats is in our jurisdiction and everything that floats is going to be organized by us. And I'm giving you fair warning of that.''

''Mr. Banks, I regret to tell you this,'' Smith said, ''Every time an international union has made an attack upon our brotherhood, our brotherhood has always come out stronger than what it was. . . . You must take that into account. If you don't know it, I'm telling you now. We'll welcome any dispute. . . .''

In September 1958, after his victory over Banks in the CPR dispute in Vancouver, Dick Greaves decided to pay a surprise visit to the NAME eastern chapter in Montreal. His first stop was at the Montreal home of NAME officer John Wood. Wood was indeed surprised—and uncomfortable. He said he couldn't talk long. ''Go and see Banks, because this is a very bad situation that has developed here,'' Wood said. Somewhat mystified by the reception he'd been given, Greaves drove to 95 Lakeshore Road, where Banks' white Eldorado was parked in the driveway. He was sure he could see Banks through the window. However, the woman who answered the door told Greaves, ''Mr. Banks is not here.''

When Greaves showed up at the NAME office at 9:00 the next morning, he found that his lock had been changed. Greaves, at that time the union's national secretary-treasurer with the power of attorney from the national president, had to wait outside the door for an hour before someone showed up and let him in.

In the early afternoon, Wood and a dozen other NAME members arrived. ''We'll call a meeting of engineers,'' Wood announced. Then he began to discuss amalgamation with Banks' SIU. It was the first Greaves had heard of the idea.

Wood repeated Banks' line about the benefits of amalgamation. It would mean support from a larger organization without sacrificing autonomy. Greaves left the room to use the washroom, and when he returned, a vote was in progress. Minutes later it was announced that the motion had passed. Members of NAME in Montreal would be called upon to vote on amalgamating with the SIU, even though there was no legal basis for the non-incorporated body to do so.

Greaves couldn't help but notice that Eastern District NAME official Peter Scragg was now packing a shoebox with him. When Scragg put down the box to visit the washroom, Greaves peaked inside. The shoebox held ballots listing alleged benefits for amalgamation. At the bottom, engineers were to mark in if they were for or against amalgamation.

Furious, Greaves rushed to see his lawyer, William Miller, who had fought Banks at his citizenship hearing. He obtained an injunction blocking Wood and Scragg, then hurried back to the office. "You're through," he cried angrily. "You are fired. You have been doing things against the interest of the engineers."

Scragg jumped up from behind the desk, grabbed Greaves, and tossed him out of the office. Bruised and cut over one eye, Greaves was warned that his title with the NAME national body meant nothing. "Little man, we've taken over here," Scragg said mockingly." Go back to the West Coast."

Scragg and Wood moved around the corner and into Banks' SIU hall. From that day on, Greaves received continuous calls at his office. Sometimes it was heavy breathing, sometimes a steady stream of abuse. When he returned to the NAME hall four days after he had been so unceremoniously ejected, he persuaded a janitor to let him in. His office was stripped bare. All the union's files were gone. Letterheads and envelopes were shredded like confetti. There wasn't even a calendar left on the wall.

The old janitor was as shocked as Greaves. "Monsieur, monsieur, I cleaned the place up. Look!" A Bell repairman followed them into the ransacked office. "I'll have the connection made very soon," he said.

"What connection?" Greaves asked.

"I have an order to connect your phone through the SIU office."

"Can I see the order?"

The work order was passed to Greaves. ''What do these hieroglyphics mean?'' he asked.

The Bell man explained that calls to the NAME office at 484 McGill Street were to be patched over the SIU switchboard, then redirected back to the NAME hall. Greaves grabbed the work order and stuffed it into his pocket. When he refused to hand it back, the Bell man ran out and returned with his foreman. ''This is the property of Bell Telephone,'' Greaves was told. ''Okay, have me arrested for a twenty-five-cent piece of paper,'' he replied.

When the foreman left, Greaves ran back down St. James Street to Miller's office. That afternoon, the Bell superintendent arrived at Greaves' office. He explained that he had been called into Banks' penthouse office the previous week and introduced to someone claiming to be a NAME official who put in the phone order.

The NAME situation continued to get worse and by the spring of 1959, Banks had been called before the Canadian Labour Congress to face raiding charges. Greaves and Banks sat across a conference table from each other at the Congress' Ottawa headquarters. With a sneer, Banks tossed a bundle of cheques onto the table. ''I had that guy on my payroll for a long time and here are the cheques to prove it,'' Banks declared.

Bill Dodge of the CLC sensed something strange. Banks was suing Greaves for a hefty sum of money which he said had been advanced to grease the takeover of NAME. Now, Banks was saying that the money was Greaves' salary. ''Aren't those the cheques which are now the basis of a court case that you now have against the NAME for the restitution of this money for your union?'' Dodge asked.

Banks was caught in a lie. His grand gesture had only looked foolish. Losing his temper, he stormed out of the room.

When found guilty of raiding by the entire CLC executive Banks refused to answer charges. The SIU was suspended from the CLC on June 18, 1959, and expelled in the April convention of 1960. For CLC unions, the suspension meant that they could organize against the SIU without penalties. For Banks, the expulsion stung. He wanted to be part of a group, not alone. Of course, the only part of the group that he wanted to be was the head. By

August 1959, the SIU was being treated as a pariah by the CLC, CBRT, steelworkers and autoworkers. But rather than try to be conciliatory, Banks announced he'd be setting up a new labour federation. Exactly who would be in the federation was never made clear, however.

Banks fantasized about being head of all Canadian union members. Some people around him felt he dreamed of using this as a stepping stone to the loftier title of Prime Minister. CLC executive members also suspected that Banks had paid higher Congress membership dues than he had to, because he wanted to create an exaggerated view of his power. Now he was a complete outcast from the Congress, which spoke for three-quarters of organized labour in Canada. His progress had been stalled and he might actually be pushed backwards. They were all his enemies. It was war.

Christmas 1959 was a joyful time for Dick Greaves. Finally, he was standing up to Hal Banks—and winning. The tide had turned in the past year when, drawn by a common disaffection for Banks, Greaves' NAME had merged with the 40,000-member CBRT. They picked the West Coast for their counterattack. Banks was at his weakest there and there wasn't much left of NAME anywhere else.

The NAME-CBRT forces enjoyed quick and heady success. By Christmas of 1959, Greaves estimates that they had taken 80 percent of Banks' west coast membership, including the prized White Pass–Yukon contract. Feeling a little cocky, he sent Banks a Christmas telegram:

HAHAHA HAL STOP
WE'VE GOT THE MEMBERS STOP
WHAT HAVE YOU GOT STOP
MERRY CHRISTMAS DICK GREAVES.

Greaves had begun getting harassing phone calls at his Pender Street West Office, the same type he had heard SIU workers make to John McGough a couple years before. But he reasoned that the threat of violence from Banks had passed. On Saturday morning,

January 30, 1960, he told sailors at the Patricia Hotel in Vancouver that the worst was over.

That afternoon Greaves received another of the unsettling calls in his office:

"Is that you Dick?"

"Yes."

The caller hung up. A few minutes later, two men showed up at his office door. One was about five foot ten and in his late twenties. Behind him stood a man about six foot four. Greaves had never seen either of them before.

"Are you Greaves?"

"Yes."

"We've come to give you something."

Greaves glanced at the shorter man's hands to see what he was going to be given. The man was wearing yellow gloves and his hands were clenched into fists. The first punch caught Greaves in the right side of his head. Since it was a Saturday and the office building was empty, no one heard him cry out.

The larger man spoke for the first time: "Shut him up." Greaves heard a bang. It was a fist hitting his skull. He felt warm blood. It reminded him of someone hitting a tomato. When the walls started to move, he knew he was falling. As he fell, he tried to land face down to protect his vital organs. At fifty years of age, he wasn't about to fight back.

When Greaves drifted back into something close to consciousness, he found himself in a taxi about two blocks from the hospital. He started to scream about gangsterism and violence and hoods, then realized the cab was organized by the Teamsters—at that time about the only union on the West Coast still supporting Banks.

It was a severe beating. Greaves ran up $3,200 in medical bills for skin grafts, as well as repairs to his cracked ribs and broken teeth. Police told him that his attackers appeared to have been wearing knuckle-dusters or holding rolls of coins. Doctors had to rebreak his nose to straighten it out; even then, it never looked the same. He was kept awake for two days because of his concussion and it wasn't until July that neurosurgeons were convinced that he had suffered no permanent brain damage.

The SIU would charge that Greaves beat himself with his own shoe for sympathy. Some CLC members, not forgiving Greaves' past closeness with the SIU, laughed at the wildly improbable story, but spread it anyway. No explanation was given for how he had managed to kick in his own ribs.

Greaves traces the beating to having put his name to the Christmas message that he sent to Banks. "I signed it, foolishly. You should never fool around with a psychopath."

13

They looked like a cartoonist's view of real American gangsters.

Don Secord of CBRT describes the appearance of Hal Banks and Seafarers' head Paul Hall.

It had been six years since Montreal lawyer John Schlesinger got his first taste of what it was like to be on the wrong side of Hal Banks. There had been the telephone calls, most of them at about two in the morning. Typically, a voice would sigh deeply, then say "Too bad, somebody's going to have to go to a funeral." But Schlesinger hadn't backed down. And now he was being offered a great deal of money to become counsel to Hal Banks and the SIU.

In 1954, it was Schlesinger who had agreed to handle the case of John Droeger in his fight against Banks' blacklist. He had been warned at the time that he could expect trouble. "Everyone else who would try to take him on had been roughed up," Schlesinger remembers. But Schlesinger, a feisty bantamweight who had concentrated most of his energies on divorce cases, said he wasn't afraid. The first thing he did after taking the case was to write Banks and ask him exactly what the Do Not Ship List was. He got his answer early the next morning when the calls began. Callers never identified themselves. They just sighed, swore, threatened or said nothing.

After a month of the "telephone treatment" Schlesinger had had enough. He would go on the attack. "I located Banks' unlisted phone number through the Bell," he remembers," and I phoned there at about three or four in the morning and he answered. I didn't know his voice but it was obviously him. . . . I identified myself. I said if these phone calls to my home don't stop by tomorrow, I said 'there's going to be a lot more than phone calls that you're going to get, Mr. Banks.' I gave my name and then hung up.'' The harassment stopped after that. Instead, Schlesinger recalls that ''I started to get occasional phone calls from people who asked me if I ever wanted to come to work for the SIU.'' But he declined, saying that he didn't want to discuss working for Banks while he was still handling cases against him.

The Droeger case was bitterly fought all the way to the Supreme Court. When it was over in 1955 and Schlesinger had won, Banks shook his hand. There had been no more threats. Banks had conducted himself as a gentleman. ''Once you stood up to Banks, he respected you,'' Schlesinger says. ''If more people had done that, there would have been far less trouble with him.''

After the Droeger victory, Schlesinger was hired by Joseph Stern, who also wanted to fight the blacklist in court. During the proceedings the attorney was fascinated by how politely Banks was now conducting himself. ''Whenever I did write to the SIU for a seaman, I'd get a personal call from Hal Banks. This amazed me. He would take time for the smallest type of case, any little matter. If he was interested in something, he would go after the smallest little thing. He'd nitpick.''

In 1960, Stern won his case. It was three years since he had been thrown off the lakes. His reward was the right to work again. Schlesinger's reward was a series of increasingly attractive job offers from the SIU. Banks wanted to surround himself with winners. He hadn't held a grudge against Jack Casper for beating him up at the San Francisco union hall and he wasn't about to hold one against Schlesinger. Banks knew talent when he saw it.

Banks offered the lawyer a $75,000 annual retainer, plus a weekly salary—a staggering amount at that time. But Schlesinger still had his doubts, so Banks invited him up to his penthouse office. The blacklist was gone, he announced. Reforms had been made. Sailors were happy now. They were being treated like human beings. No longer did they have to slide about on icy decks, eat disgusting food or sleep on hard bunks in cramped cabins. Shippers either treated them well or answered to Hal C. Banks. To demonstrate, Schlesinger recalls,''he got on the phone with several of these people from these steamship companies and he spoke with them. I listened on the open line and he kept telling them how he wanted this improved and that improved, the food improved and all that.''

Schlesinger knew a sales pitch when he heard one, but he did believe Banks was sincere in his desire for improvements so he agreed to come aboard on a piecework basis, rejecting the attractive retainer offer. As a professional courtesy, however, Schlesinger spoke with Banks' counsel, the imposing John Ahern.

When told of Banks' offer, Ahern, a proud man, was obviously deflated. ''Well, perhaps he feels that I'm too old,'' he said.

''I don't think it's that,'' Schlesinger replied. ''I figured that perhaps he'll neutralize me by engaging me.''

Nevertheless, Ahern was shunted to the sidelines, and Banks doted on his new star. Whenever Banks saw Schlesinger's car parked in front of the union hall, he'd say, ''You need a new car,'' and then offer to buy him one. The offer was at once affectionate and corrupt, as the car would be paid for with union funds. Schlesinger, who drove a less gaudy Cadillac than Banks, declined.

''The first thing that Hal Banks did was take me down to a convention in Puerto Rico. . . . He had never asked Ahern to go on any conventions and Ahern had done yeoman work with him. Wonderful work with him. And yet he never did. Well, I didn't know this. Ahern learned that Hal had invited me to go to the convention and not him, he felt it very keenly. He felt very bad about it and I felt very bad about it.''

Schlesinger would soon learn how much Banks loved conventions. Earlier, at the International Transport Workers Federation (ITF) convention in Berne, Switzerland, he had shared the spotlight with the top executive officers of the SIU such as Paul Hall. These international conventions were a chance for the Seafarers to strut. They'd be met at the airport by a fleet of black limousines, then whisked off to the best hotel in the city. All eyes would be on them as they swept into the lobby, their fleshy midsections draped in expensive mohair and their flanks guarded by hulking sociopaths. That was worth the trip alone to Hal Banks. Others, like CBRT secretary Don Secord, would view the spectacle with a mixture of disgust and humour. When he saw Paul Hall and Banks together, he was struck by how they ''looked as though they were brothers. Fat slobs. They looked like a cartoonist's version of real American gangsters.'' Secord and the CBRT were determined that if the SIU were to command attention at the ITF convention in June 1960, it would be for a different reason. So the CBRT used the occasion to charge that Banks was a thug and that he and the SIU didn't deserve to belong to the eighty-nation federation.

Banks responded with unctuous good humour at an ITF luncheon, where he sat next to Secord. He didn't appear to hold a grudge, but when the luncheon ended he summoned three of his men to his hotel room. He ordered them to pummel Secord.

''Do you know who that guy was sitting beside you?'' Banks asked lieutenant Michael Sheehan. ''That is that fucking bastard from the CB of RT. We're going to dump that bastard.''

With Sheehan were Banks' bodyguard Roman Gralewicz and Paul Hall's protector, a shifty little man named Bobby. After receiving their instructions, they located Secord and followed him to his hotel. When they discovered that they could get a room next to his, they reported back to Banks who gave the order to ''kick the shit out of him.''

By that time, Sheehan was getting nervous. ''You are crazy, man,'' he protested. ''If there is any trouble here, where the hell will we get out? There is no trains or planes, only mountains. . . .''

Planning to beat up Secord wasn't an intelligent response to his charges of gangsterism. Banks knew this. But on another level, that made the idea more appealing. The very audacity of the attack would have given him a primitive satisfaction.

Secord remembers that Banks was a clever man but ''an egotist of the first order. He believed that he could get away with anything, that money would buy anybody.'' If he could beat murder raps, then surely a hotel room beating was not out of his power. The very improbability and brazenness would fuel Banks' aura. He was above the law everywhere else he went, or so it seemed. Why not Switzerland too? That would make him a truly international hood.

But Banks either backed off or was called off by Hall. At home in Montreal, there'd be better opportunities to bash CBRT men. The assault in Switzerland never took place.

The CBRT-prompted investigation into Banks paid off and the SIU was expelled from the ITF. In three months he had been kicked out of two major labour federations. By the time he reached the Puerto Rico convention, however, his ego seems to have rallied.

Banks' trip to the convention with Schlesinger was to be a happier occasion. He was in full strut, leaving the impression he owned Puerto Rico. And while he was supposed to be there for union business—including a fight between the AFL-CIO Maritime Trades Department and the Teamsters—Banks would later report that he was also studying recreation for Seafarers and organizing a brassiere factory.

The trip had been arranged as part of a flurry of activity to bolster Banks' prestige inside the SIU after his Canadian Labour Congress expulsion. He won a post as vice-president of the AFL-CIO Maritime Trades Department, which made him the organization's ranking member on the Great Lakes.

Banks would report back to his union that he had made a side trip to Cuba, where he met with Fidel Castro. Apparently, Canada's anti-communist crusader saw no incongruity in dealing with a communist. He would brag in years to come that Castro had been a guest at both his Lakeshore Road home and his Drummond Street apartment. As Castro did visit Canada in 1959, the visit is not inconceivable. And when later visitors came to Banks' house, the man who had thrown thousands of sailors out of work on the charge of being communist would proudly display two drab white lamps which he boasted were gifts from Castro.

The southern sojourn lasted almost four months and, according to a former Banks' lieutenant, almost bankrupted the Seafarers' Canadian District. (Later, to make up the loss, Banks would simply blacklist more sailors, making room for new members and their initiation fees.) The costs were, no doubt, enormous. Banks skippered a luxurious yacht while in Puerto Rico, which

The young Hal Banks would have known this Richmond, California vantage point as Nichol's Knob. From it, one can see the huge Chevron refinery, operated by Standard Oil when Banks was a west coast tankerman, and with a slight turn of the head, some of the most exclusive homes in the United States.

Above left: Hal Banks in 1954, the year the federal Liberal government overturned a deportation order against him.

Below left: Hal Banks (centre) is given a plaque for ''meritorious service to the labor movement'' in 1962 by the Maritimes Trades Department of the American Federation of Labor—Confederation of Industrial Organizations (AFO–CIO) in the United States. Banks is flanked by U.S. labor leaders Peter McGavin (left) and Paul Hall (right).

Above: Hal Banks appears impatient with the proceedings during his January 1963 testimony before the Norris Commission.

Hal Banks urges SIU members to stay off the job to protest a federal trusteeship of maritime unions, October 1963.

Hal Banks and Seafarers' lawyer Joe Nuss (left) discuss their case before the Norris Commission, January 1963.

SIU members gather on Parliament Hill to protest Ottawa's proposed trusteeship of maritime unions in the wake of the Norris Commission report, October 1963.

Hal Banks munches a fish sandwich from a truck loaded with 10,000 sandwiches for SIU protesters in Ottawa, October 1963.

A bailiff, trying (in vain) to deliver a writ of arrest on Hal Banks at his Pointe Claire home on July 22, 1964, is told to move his car by a policeman.

Hal Banks (left) flees the camera of *Toronto Star* reporter Robert Reguly after being discovered on a Seafarers' dock in Brooklyn, N.Y. Both Canadian and U.S. authorities had stated that Banks could not be found. Seconds after the picture was taken, Reguly was clubbed on the head and chased by SIU members.

Hal Banks (right) sits in a Montreal courtroom in 1964, awaiting judgment on a charge of conspiracy to wound, maim or disfigure Captain Henry Walsh.

Hal Banks is handcuffed to a Quebec Provincial Police officer after he has been sentenced to five years in prison for the beating of Captain Henry Walsh, May 1964. Two weeks later, released on bail, he fled to the United States and never returned to Canada.

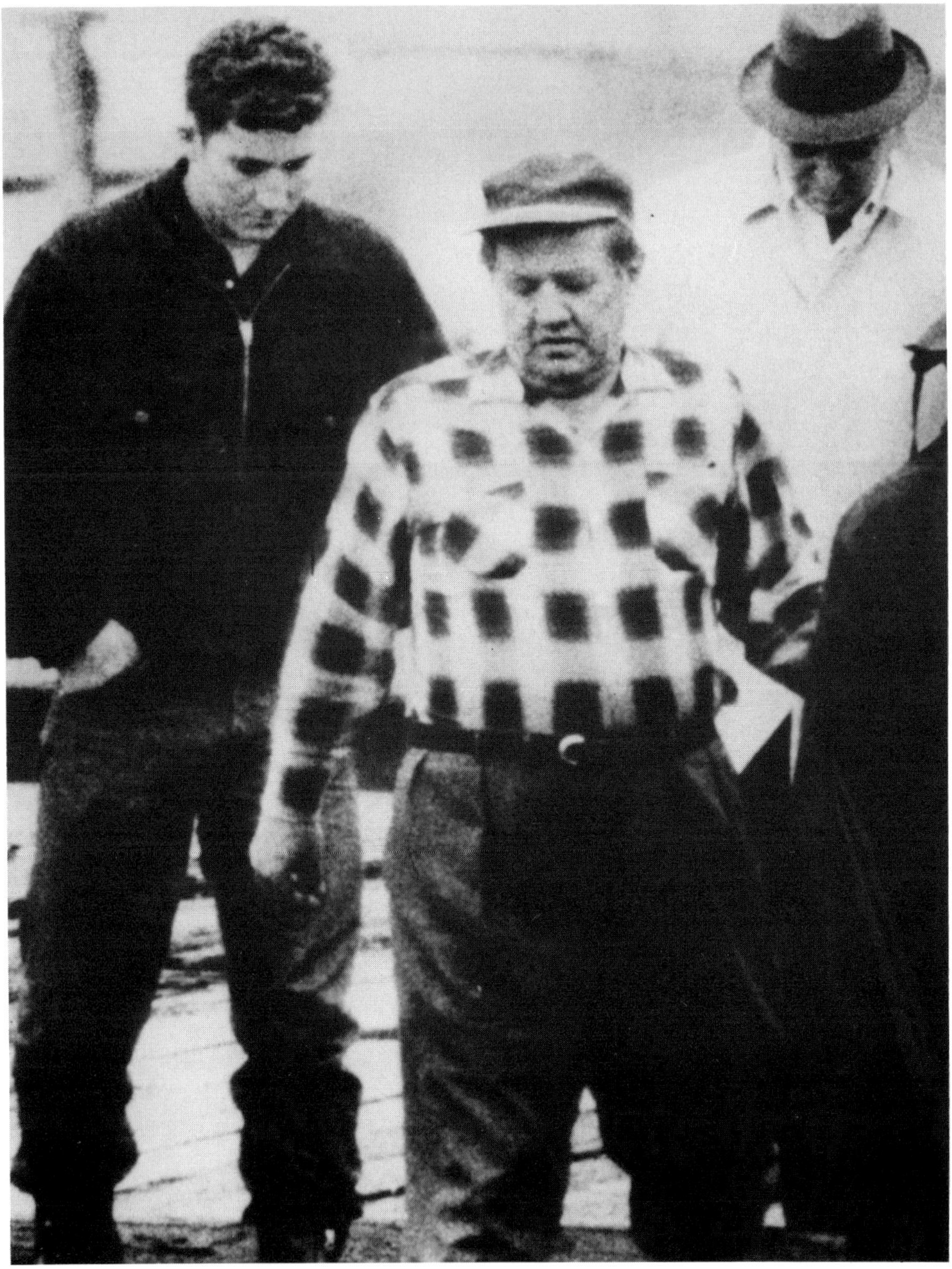

Hal Banks (centre), deposed SIU head, steps onto a Brooklyn dock in 1964, where a Seafarers' yacht is moored. Banks was served with a subpoena in connection with a lawsuit by Upper Lakes Shipping.

Handcuffed and haggard, Hal Banks appears at a 1967 New York City extradition proceeding.

Roman Gralewicz, President of the SIU, tells a 1975 Montreal press conference that a review board will ''take some of the sting'' out of charges of waterfront corruption.

Hal Banks lived aboard the *Malabar* at this San Francisco marina in the early 1980s. Alcatraz looms in the background.

More than two decades after Banks fled Canada, the basement bar of his Pointe Claire house remains intact.

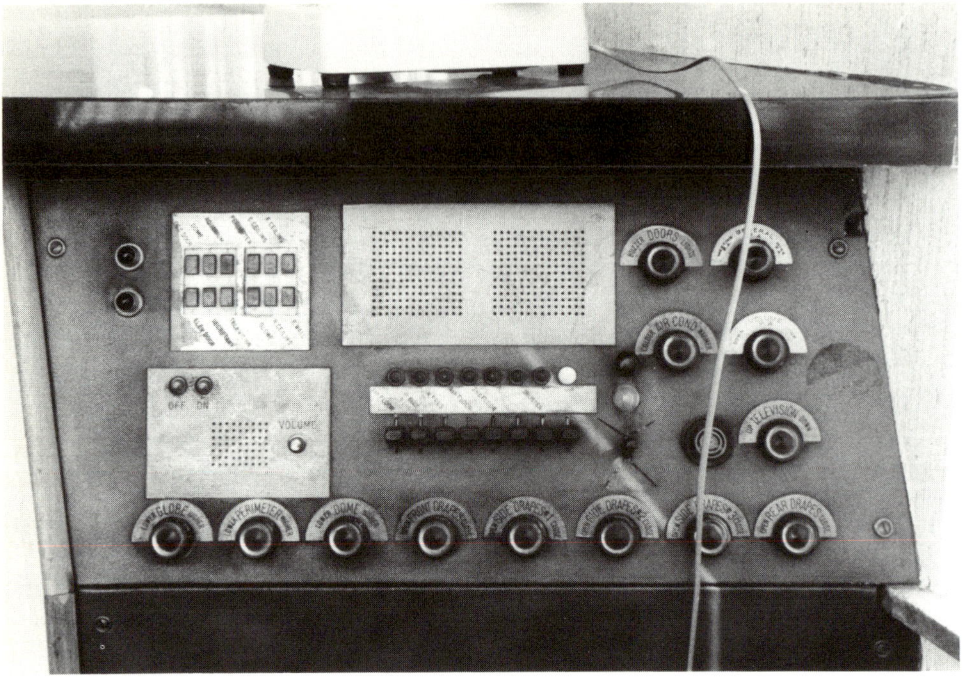

By pushing buttons on the infamous control panel in his fortress-like Montreal office, Hal Banks could listen in on conversations throughout the building, lock doors (including the doors of his private elevator), and lower an overhead dome to make his voice sound deeper.

San Francisco boatyard workers restore the *Malabar* in June 1986, nine months after Banks sold it to the Sailors' Union of the Pacific.

he treated as his own. And, of course, it was essential that he ship his white Cadillac convertible down from Montreal. "I couldn't get one of that quality," he'd explain. "Can you imagine me getting into one of those little French cars? I couldn't get underneath the steering wheel."

Schlesinger warned Banks that he shouldn't drink, since he might lose the respect of his peers. Banks growled, "Once a year," and the discussion was closed. Schlesinger remembers that most of the time Banks "never drank, never. I've been with him [when] he'd order wine for me and never touch it. Once a year, at a convention, he'd break loose. . . . It was over just like a rainfall and then stopped dead. He was a very determined person and very controlled."

The Puerto Rico trip was part of a testing process for Schlesinger, and he felt that Banks was trying to get something on him that more or less could put him in his control, as he had with others. Those others, Banks would brag, included members of the Liberal cabinet, whom he had claimed to have set up with prostitutes, then photographed.

When Schlesinger didn't give in, Banks took a new tack. He decided that his new lawyer was a prude and began acting in kind. In Schlesinger's presence, "he never once made a pass or said anything . . . about or to a woman." In other company, however, Banks was less ascetic. And later he would recount to a less squeamish friend that during his four months in Puerto Rico, he had enjoyed the best orgasm of his life—courtesy of a skilled hooker, 200 feet of string and a nimble, trained dog.

It was perhaps a measure of his fundamental insecurity that Banks so badly wanted to earn Schlesinger's respect. Unable to give him costly gifts, he impressed him by giving a lot money to others incognito. Of course, many times it was union funds he was using but he was occasionally known to be generous.

He was also generous to himself. Banks once asked Schlesinger why he work dark suits on hot summer days. Schlesinger replied that formal appearance can give a businessman an edge. From then on, the dozens of suits that Banks ordered every year from his tailor were invariably dark and expensive. In fact, Banks didn't just buy dark suits, he stockpiled them. His future wife Marija would claim he had 300 expensive suits with which he could choose to wear one of his 150 dress shirts. Apparently he wasn't so fussy about shoes, as they numbered only in the dozens.

Beneath it all Schlesinger sensed Banks' insecurity: "All those executives in the various companies and those people in the government used to make him feel inferior, so he overdid it by overreacting and acting superior. Because he had the power. If he was talking to somebody from one of the shipping lines [on the telephone], he'd sit there and wink at me when he was talking to them. He'd be telling them what to do, ordering them. And I knew that he felt in his heart that he was socially and educationally inferior to them."

Nevertheless Schlesinger couldn't help but be astounded at the ease with which Banks could press a button to get in touch with Ottawa and speak with some of the very lowest to the very highest. Asked if this would reach the prime minister's office, Schlesinger recalls only that it was "High, high. That's all I can tell you. He would get them immediately. There wasn't anyone who said he was busy. When he'd call, he'd get through. And he'd do the same when he'd call Washington or San Francisco. . . . Sometimes it horrified me to think that a man could have that much power without being elected."

There was also the occasional allusion to people who had gone missing from the waterfront. Banks' tone and expression suggested he knew how the person had disappeared. But he wasn't a man to reflect on such events. For him, lawbreaking was a right, not a transgression. "Hal was always sure of himself, as he had every right to be because he had the power," Schlesinger said. ". . . Don't forget, Hal was put in there by the greatest authority in Canada and as such, nobody could touch him. Hal Banks was an autocrat. He thought he had a right—he really, honestly and truly felt he had a right to know what was going on in his organization. . . . He was very careful that the men were kept under control. . . . He wanted to keep his union—he used to call it—clean. That word clean turned up fifty times in a conversation."

Keeping things clean meant spying into washrooms at the St. James Street union hall. Schlesinger remembers that Banks could "see anyone do anything in that building, even in the bathrooms

. . . because a lot of the men, when they want to talk, they go to the men's room. . . . But he had the damn room bugged and had a TV camera on them. . . . It was all taped. And then he'd get the man up [to his office]. . . . When he had something against him, he'd call him up. . . . And he'd play the damn tape back to him and the poor guy would shrivel up.''

Keeping things clean also meant spying outside his union hall, Schlesinger said: ''I don't think there was any shipping company that didn't have in their employ—unknowingly—people who were reporting back to Banks.''

Former union officer Norm Cunningham was probably one of the few men who benefited from Banks' love of the tape recorder. Arguably the second most powerful man in the Canadian District of the SIU, he left the union in 1960. Depending on whom you believe, Cunningham quit because he was furious that Banks had lied to him in denying the expulsion of the SIU from the CLC, or because Banks saw him as a threat to his power, and squeezed him out by stopping his paycheques.

Cunningham had lived largely free from Banks' interference since the early 1950s with Harry Lundeberg's blessing. More than once, Lundeberg had got on the phone and told Banks to leave Cunningham alone.

With Lundeberg dead, the buffer between Banks and Cunningham was gone, and Cunningham recognized his vulnerability. But he did have piles of taped messages that Banks had sent to him in happier days in envelopes marked ''Private and Confidential.'' (Banks said he didn't trust his secretaries enough to dictate letters.) And although they had an agreement to destroy the tapes once they had been listened to, Cunningham had kept his as insurance. Soon after leaving the union, it was reported that Cunningham had a safe full of tapes, two shotguns and a .32 Colt automatic pistol in case anyone came for him or the tapes.

14

We have no alternative.

A shipper explains why he gave in to Banks

Hal Banks demanded a show of respect; an acknowledgement that he was in charge and that he was nobody's patsy. As proof that he answered to nobody, he loved to tell of the time a Great Lakes shipper had offered to double his salary and make him personnel manager.

"When are you going to kiss me?" Banks said.

"What?"

"When are you going to kiss me?"

"Kiss you?"

"Ya, kiss me. I like to get kissed when I'm getting fucked."

Banks loved to make shippers squirm. It showed how much they needed him. It showed who held the real power. And if they needed to be reminded, Banks could let shippers know he wasn't just boss of the Canadian District of the SIU, he was also Ottawa's chosen boy. He refreshed their memories about the ease with which he could call mandarins in Ottawa; nobody in power dared put Hal Banks on hold. It was a commonly held opinion on the waterfront that Banks could make certain Cabinet ministers squirm more than others. All it took was a brown manila envelope, a stamp, and a photograph taken in Banks' Drummond Street apartment.

Jack Leitch, head of Upper Lakes Shipping, would hear lurid reports from friends who had had to negotiate with Banks. Banks bragged that at least one Cabinet minister was part of the SIU's "Ottawa branch."

No doubt Banks would have enjoyed having a few compromising photos of Leitch, since Upper Lakes was not one of his favourite shipping companies. From the very beginning, Upper Lakes had argued that it was the members' choice which union they joined. Canada Steamship Lines, which helped bring Banks into Canada, followed an opposite tack. They signed with Banks first, then let the men fall into line. Other shippers either complied and rubber-stamped contracts with the SIU, or they let CSL suck up even more of the shipping business.

Shipping was and is a fiercely competitive business and Canada Steamship Lines president Rodgie McLagan wasn't the type of man to let ethics get in the way of profits. The shipping season was limited and a tied-up ship cost about $5,000 a day. It was the government's job to lay down the law. And if the government could be tricked, that was its fault for not being more clever. So when the CSL decided to shift its fleet from the Canadian to the Bermudian flag—thus avoiding up to $98 million a year in taxes—McLagan didn't question the ethics of his move. Neither did Banks. As he explained it to his members, somehow it seemed the patriotic thing to do: "Of course we were taking a chance in going along with this but we feel that our economic strength is such that our risks are considerably minimized in comparison with the greater security we would obtain if the company succeeds in making the Canadian government extend protection to our domestic shipping by this move."

Canada Steamship Lines was the largest member of the Association of Lakes Carriers and, as such, insured that Banks was invulnerable to any action that it might take against him. Unified sanctions against Banks were, to say the least, difficult when CSL was busy buying gifts for Banks and trying to get him into exclusive country clubs. As Jack Leitch recalls, "There were then about a dozen companies. Usually they'd have a great meeting and everybody would meet for two or three days and then you'd come out and find out that an agreement had been made a few hours before between Banks [and] . . . McLagan. It broke down frequently."

Banks let the shippers know they couldn't hide from him

behind legalities and contracts. There was always the threat of a "prayer meeting," a term Banks loved for illegal walkouts. (He reasoned that its connotations of piety would hold a natural appeal to his French-Canadian members.) But Canada Steamship Lines had never needed threats or coaxing. In 1959, CSL personnel manager William Dunkerley had told Dick Greaves that his company wasn't going to honour its collective agreement for marine engineers with Greaves' NAME union. Instead, they had signed a new agreement with Banks.

When Greaves pointed out that this was clearly illegal, Dunkerley seemed unconcerned. "Did you read the statement I made a couple of days ago before our management associations?" he asked. "There are no teeth in the labour laws. Have a look at the Act. First of all you have to go to the minister and get permission to prosecute. That will take you a couple of months. We will kick it around in the courts here for a year and if necessary we will take it to the Supreme Court of Canada. This will take about two years." And even if they should lose, Dunkerley added, the penalty would just be a fine. CSL had received an "assurance from Mr. Banks of indemnifications. By this time you'll be out of business if you do not get your dues coming in. You know that. That is the way of life."

Pressure was enormous for other shippers to follow the CSL lead. In April 1959, Scott Misener Steamships Ltd. also broke its NAME contract. The company explained its motivations in a letter to Bernard Wilson, director of industrial relations for the Department of Labour:

> Dear Mr Wilson:
>
> This is to inform you that Scott Misener Steamships Limited and Misener Holdings Limited have signed an agreement with the Seafarers' International Union of North America—Licensed Division.
>
> This, of course we realize is against the Labour Relations Act, but under the circumstances that I have explained to you, we have no alternative but to do so. There is also a copy enclosed of a letter from Mr. Banks indemnifying our Companies from any lawsuits, etc. that may arise out of this agreement.

By 1960, the Association of Lake Carriers was sinking fast. Its president, also a vice-president of Canada Steamship Lines, announced he was quitting and taking his company with him. Three other lines, La Vérendrye Lines, Beaconsfield Steamships and Mohawk Navigation, followed suit. By June 1961, two more shippers had dropped out, leaving just N.M. Paterson and Sons Ltd., Carryore Limited and Upper Lakes Shipping Limited. Banks refused to deal with them as an association, demanding that each shipper deal with him separately.

Jack Leitch was in the middle of a war. With Banks' new power in the AFL-CIO Maritime Trades Department, he could draw support from the Teamsters and International Longshoremen's Association on the South Lakes. Leitch estimated his shipping line would be forced out of business in a year if his ships were shut down. With Banks' support south of the border, that was a real possibility. Already, the delays caused by SIU pickets in 1961 of the *Wheat King, Northern Venture* and *Hilda Marjanne* had cost Upper Lakes almost $375,000. Now their vessels would sail under armed guard. Leitch paid $361,000 to the Citadel Detective agency in Montreal for protection. Obscene, threatening calls came into the Upper Lakes office. Leitch also got them at home, as did his personnel manager, Thomas Houtman. At the height of the threats, a guard watched Leitch's Toronto home and another Citadel man guarded Houtman's young daughter.

The Upper Lakes contract was due to expire with the SIU in the 1962 season. Leitch signed with the newly formed Canadian Maritime Union, headed by former Banks strongman Michael Sheehan. The CMU was formed in October 1961 after William Smith of the CBRT requested a meeting with Canadian Labour Congress president Claude Jodoin and secretary-treasurer Donald Macdonald. Also present was CLC vice-president Bill Dodge, who recalls that Smith said he was willing to turn over the CBRT's entire membership of Upper Lakes Shipping if the Congress would assume responsibility for the conduct of its affairs from that time forward. It was accepted and now replaced the CBRT as the arch enemy of the SIU. Now, instead of leading the Canadian Labour Congress, Banks was fighting its million-plus members. Certifications won by the CMU with Upper Lakes weren't about to make him back off.

Gustav Strathie liked to keep to himself. The sixty-two-year-old recluse lived alone, having never married. He didn't have any enemies that he knew of, and people seldom came to his home. The few times that they did, he would peek outside and make sure everything was all right before opening the door.

But he had a momentary lapse on March 16, 1962, when a stranger called at his Vancouver home shortly after 7:00 p.m. The stranger didn't say word to Strathie. He just pulled out a .38-calibre police special and began to pistol-whip him. Even without the gun, Strathie was no match for the younger stranger, who stood six foot three and weighed 260 pounds.

The man must have cracked Strathie a dozen times with the pistol, pushing him down the hallway. When they reached the end of the hall, the pistol was momentarily jammed against Strathie's groin. The stranger had been holding the .38 by the barrel in his gloved fist, so that he could hammer him with its handle.

Strathie grabbed the pistol and fired one shot up into the man's chest. He gave a grunt of surprise and fell.

''Who the hell are you anyway?'' Strathie asked. There was no answer, only the groans of a dying man. Another stranger rushed into the home but turned tail when Strathie fired a blast in his direction.

The dead man was Clayton ''Mike'' Stratton, longtime friend of SIU west coast boss Rod Heinekey, and a man of violent habits. When police checked his apartment, they found an assortment of blasting caps and dynamite. And when they checked a little more into his background, they discovered that he was out on bail after a picket-line assault the month before.

The Teamster Hall had been picketed by the Retail-Wholesale and Department Store Union and Stratton had been on his way to the hall to see his friend Heinekey. He beat up two pickets on the line. They said it was unprovoked. He said they tried to stop him from entering the hall, so he flattened them. Either way, it appeared that on the night of the beating, Stratton and his cohort set out to silence a witness in the picket-line beating. They got addresses mixed up and ended up at the home of Strathie, a complete stranger who had nothing at all to do with the SIU. The muddle had cost Stratton his life.

Jimmy Todd felt a jolt when he read of the Stratton shooting. Back in 1949, when he was working as an organizer for the SIU on the West Coast, he was attacked by a Canadian Seamen's Union gang on board a Canadian Pacific Railway ferry. When he had informed Banks of the attack, he was told that he'd be provided with a bodyguard. Within a few days, Todd's guard arrived from Seattle. His name was Clayton "Mike" Stratton.

With the formation of the Canadian Maritime Union Jimmy Todd had returned to the waterfront. Todd had been working at the Toronto De Havilland plant since his unsuccessful fight against Banks' DNS list in 1952. He signed on with the CMU as secretary-treasurer for $400 a month and the opportunity to fight Banks again.

Strange phone calls at his home started up almost immediately. When Todd was on the road, he worried about his wife Agnes and their baby daughter. One night when he was away, a stranger called to say that Todd's car had been run off the road. Agnes was told her husband was lying by the highway, injured and alone.

The call was a hoax but the Todds decided that Agnes should take the baby and go visit her parents in Scotland. She stayed away for four months, but less than a week after she returned, Agnes heard two strangers threatening her husband at the entrance to their apartment. It was a Friday and Agnes was in the kitchen cooking fish. A hot vat of grease was on the stove. She remembers thinking, "Well, I'll let them see we have some weapons. I may not have a baseball bat but I've got some hot fat here! So I put my baby in her highchair and went around to the other side of the kitchen from where they were standing and asked them if they were staying for supper. And Jim said, 'They are no friends of mine.' I said, 'Well, in that case, they'll be leaving right now' . . ."

The strangers left. A couple of weeks later, Todd suspected

another attack was in the works. He and Bill England of the Canadian Labour Congress were preparing to drive up to Port McNicoll, Ontario, for a ratification meeting on two Canadian Pacific ships. Calls kept coming into the CLC Toronto office asking if they had left for the meeting.

Todd decided they shouldn't risk staying in Port McNicoll overnight. Driving home after the meeting, Todd and England noticed a Corvair and a Rambler following them at high speed. Todd accelerated up to ninety miles an hour, but the Corvair passed them. Now Todd and England were sandwiched between the cars. Todd sped up. The Corvair sped up. Todd slowed down. The Corvair slowed down. He worried that he was going to be run off the road. So he floored the gas pedal and passed the Corvair at 100 miles an hour on the right-hand shoulder, then raced towards the Ontario Provincial Police station at the north end of Barrie. When his pursuers saw where he was heading, they veered off towards Camp Borden.

When the OPP stopped two cars full of men later that night, Todd and England were called to identify them. At the wheel of the Corvair was Paul Gagne, vice-president of the SIU.

15

It is highly probable that physical violence will be resorted to if found expedient.

RCMP report warns the Justice Minister of waterfront tensions

Hal Banks loved to conquer, but ruling didn't come as naturally. He had no trouble winning wives or mistresses, or gaining leverage over associates, but the give-and-take of life after the conquest was foreign to him. Lawyer John Schlesinger recalls that Banks "was not a great settler. . . . He was a good negotiator, as long as he kept his position of superiority. But when you settle, the other person gets something too, which is what he didn't want."

Schlesinger traces Banks' downfall to a dinner at the Château Laurier hotel in Ottawa. The SIU had been fighting a shipper before the Canada Labour Relations Board. At one table sat Schlesinger and Banks' taciturn right-hand man, Red McLaughlin. At a nearby table was the head of the shipping line, his lawyer and a handful of executives. Banks wasn't present: As was his custom, he left Canada Labour Relations Board hearings to Schlesinger and McLaughlin.

Schlesinger remembers turning to McLaughlin that evening and saying: "You know, Red, I don't think that this hearing should go on. I think that we've won our point and all that we're doing now is beating a dead horse. You know you're going to win this hearing. Why don't I go over and speak to Mr. So and So of this particular steamship line, and say to him, 'Enough is enough. We know that you know that we're winning this thing. Why don't we just shake hands, make peace, and come to an agreement? And then follow it up with a written agreement.' " McLaughlin didn't say a word. He just stared at Schlesinger.

Taking the silence for agreement, Schlesinger then stood up and McLaughlin shifted his chair to let him pass.

"I think you're absolutely right," Schlesinger recalls the shipowner saying when Schlesinger walked over to his table. "This is the first time any of Hal Banks' lawyers ever have made a move like this. I think it's high time we do make peace. Fine, you suggest to your boss over there, Mr. McLaughlin, you tell him that any time he's ready to walk over to this table or have me walk over to his table, we can make peace right off."

Schlesinger was delighted and returned to McLaughlin. But Banks' lieutenant just finished his meal without saying a word. There would be no peace agreement.

Stella Scavarelli didn't like the look of the two strangers at the back door of her Fort William, Ontario, home. It was 9:45 on the evening of May 21, 1962, and her husband was resting up for a night shift.

The two men wanted to speak to her husband Alfred, a general foreman for Upper Lakes shipping at their Fort William terminal, which had been picketed by SIU sympathizers when Upper Lakes ships stopped in.

"It is very important," one of the men insisted. "We have to see him. Could we go upstairs and see him?"

Definitely not, she replied.

"Maybe we will come back tomorrow at the same time," the taller of the strangers said.

"No, we would like to see him right now," his partner corrected.

She started to head upstairs to see her husband, stopping first in the kitchen to talk with her niece, who was visiting with her three-year-old girl and two-year-old boy. "Those men outside don't look good to me," Mrs. Scavarelli said. "Hang on to that phone and call the police in case anything happens."

Stella repeated to her husband that the strangers didn't look right to her. Alfred wasn't too concerned, reporting that they could be a couple of guys looking for a job. But when he came through the kitchen behind his wife, the strangers spotted him and bolted in through the back door, kicking the Scavarelli's four-year-old daughter out of the way in their charge.

Both men were carrying pick handles. Mrs. Scavarelli tackled one, but he broke away and they set upon her husband. Within minutes, his head was split open and he was lying on the floor, defenceless under a hail of kicks and clubbings. In the midst of the violence, the shorter attacker paused to correct the way his partner swung his pick handle: "Give me that goddamn axe handle and I'll kill the son-of-a-bitch," he shouted.

The taller attacker fled out the door when he saw the ugly gash on Alfred's scalp. The other man kept kicking Scavarelli in front of his wife and crying little girl. The other children heard the screaming and rushed in.

It was only when Stella Scavarelli screamed for her teenage nephews that the man fled. She threw his pick handle at him, then a chair, which she thought might have hit him because he was bleeding. Dishes that had been piled on the kitchen table were smashed. There was a hole in the ceiling from a swinging axe handle.

Scavarelli suffered permanent damage to his legs, an ugly deep scalp cut and bruises all over his body. "I might have some enemies, but I do not think that enemies would do a thing like that," he would say. "I have faced up man to man before, but I have never had any of the goddarned stuff until now."

Jack Leitch of Upper Lakes says that he was the shipper whom John Schlesinger approached with his peace proposal in the dining room of the Château Laurier. He recalls that what Schlesinger wanted to do was "settle the whole [thing on the] basis that we plop right back into the SIU. And that Banks had become a much more human person—that he understood where he had gone wrong. That he was even studying French. He [Schlesinger] was just pointing out that he [Banks] had realized the error of his ways and that he wanted to live in Montreal forever and be integrated into the city. I remember bursting out laughing at the time. . . . The basis of the problems in my estimation was—whether Banks was studying French or whatever he was doing

—that now, having taken him on once, it would be just a matter of months before he would put us on our knees. We would have been so discriminated against, I don't know what we would have had to do then."

Leitch claims he wasn't willing to settle with Schlesinger and McLaughlin. "There was no way that I could accept what he was proposing. What he was proposing was that Banks should take over the company again. . . . I think what I might have said was 'well, if he'd like to discuss it sometime, I'd be glad to do so, but I don't know what we can do.' That would be as far as I could have gone."

The day after the Château peace proposal, Banks summoned Schlesinger into his office.

"This is the end of our association," Banks announced. "You're a quisling. A quisling."

Schlesinger asked if Banks was talking about his attempt to settle with the shipowner.

"Yes."

"If that's how you feel, goodbye."

That was the last time Schlesinger spoke to Banks. He often thought Banks hadn't expected him to walk out. Sometimes he thought of the bloodshed and hundreds of thousands of dollars lost because Banks wasn't willing to settle peacefully. But with Banks there was no middle ground, Schlesinger remembers: "You were either his friend or his enemy. Period. I then became his enemy because I had spoken to the opposition."

Fred Neubauer thought he heard someone in the outer office of the Lake Sailors' Union in Cleveland. He checked, but found no one. A couple of minutes later, Neubauer and an office official thought they could hear someone rustling again. Again, they found no one. It was May 2, 1962, and everyone working for Lake Sailors' Union, Local 7000, had reason to be edgy. The United Steelworkers' affiliate wasn't just defying the SIU Canadian District, they were urging other American unionists to do the same and observe strict neutrality in the SIU-CMU battle.

Hal Banks didn't believe in neutrality and so Neubauer's union members were his enemies. And it hadn't helped the situation that Neubauer had recently written in a union publication that Banks behaved like a gangster and that his boss Paul Hall would befriend anyone who'd increase his own power, including communists and shipowners.

Neubauer left the office and drove home without incident. But while he was cooking supper, a man showed up at his home. The same man had been at the office that afternoon, insisting upon a job although employment was scarce. The stranger kept calling Neubauer "sir" and asking for something called a "waiver."

"There is no such animal to my knowledge," Neubauer said.

"Well, how can I get a job? I know I need something more."

"Well, I can give you a list of the various personnel officers to go to tomorrow. Why do you not stop in at the office tomorow and pick up one of the lists?"

"I have my wife and kids waiting here and I'm in an awful hurry," the man said in an accent that struck Neubauer as vaguely French-Canadian.

At first, Neubauer was slightly annoyed at the imposition of the stranger disturbing him at his home to talk business. Then he softened, thinking, "No, let's be considerate; let's help the man out." So he invited the stranger in, and even apologized for the sloppy condition of his home. Then he started drawing up a list of where the man might apply for work. The stranger sat unusually close to him.

"Well, he wants to see what I am writing," Neubauer thought. "I suppose if I were he, I would be curious too." Neubauer turned towards the man to explain where he'd locate one particular address. The stranger's eyes shifted and his nostrils flared. The next thing Neubauer saw was the stranger reaching under his coat and pulling out a steel crowbar.

The first two blows were to Neubauer's face—one on either side. When he tried to rise up from his chair, he was bashed across the shoulder. Before he could stand again he felt a sickening sensation. The man smashed him twice across the kneecaps, then clubbed him a couple more times across the shins for good measure.

Twenty-eight days in the hospital weren't enough to repair the damage to Neubauer's left knee, which had been shattered into small pieces. The damage to his left knee wasn't confined to the pulverized kneecap. Sixteen stitches reattached the scalp that had been torn apart. Doctors told Neubauer there were blood clots forming in his left leg. One clot broke free and lodged itself in his lung, causing permanent damage.

Captain John Bissette's wife didn't want to go to downtown Toledo on the afternoon of June 19, 1962, but he talked her into it. She had accompanied him on the Upper Lakes ship *Victorious* on its run to Toledo. A load of corn was about halfway unloaded and a cloud of corndust filled the air. ''Well, let's go,'' Bissette said. ''We'll take a run uptown and get away from this dust for a couple of hours.''

The Bissettes hailed a taxi for uptown. Halfway through their trip, the dispatcher called and asked for the cab in which the captain of the *Victorious* was riding.

''Number sixty-four,'' their driver said.

''Okay,'' the dispatcher said, and the conversation ended.

The Bissettes were dropped off at Lasalle's department store. Shortly before five, Bissette told his wife they should head back to the ship, since it would be unloaded by six. They had passed through the first set of the double doors in the Lasalles' vestibule when a voice from behind said, ''Oh, you're the captain of the Canadian ship.'' Bissette turned, catching a glimpse of a heavily built man about six foot five, then felt an oversized fist slam into his jaw, knocking out a couple of teeth. Bissette's last memory before he passed out was of the huge man stomping upon his chest. Mrs. Bissette, who saw the attack at close range, fainted from shock.

Bissette needed five stitches to close the gash in his lip, and hospital officials thought the couple would be wise to spend the night in hospital. They refused. As Bissette explained later, ''Well, it got into my head, why would anybody want to beat me up? I have got no enemies that I know of. I haven't done anything to anybody. I don't belong to a union. So the only reason I could think of was that they figured on beating me up to put me in the hospital so I couldn't take the ship out. And if I couldn't take the ship out there, the ship would be held for at least three days to get another man to bring her out."

The Bissettes boarded an ambulance for the *Victorious*, escorted by police. Half an hour after boarding, when his wife had settled into her cabin, Bissette called the mates together on the bridge.

"What are we going to do?" he was asked.

"I am going to take her out provided somebody rings the telegraph."

And so the *Victorious* sailed back to Canada, Bissette's right arm too weak from the beating to ring the telegraph bell. When he arrived in Toronto two days later, he learned he had a fractured bone under his eye. His doctor told him he had never seen a man get so badly beaten up without having more bones broken. Even so, it was three months before Bissette could chew with any force on the right side of his mouth.

It was the *Victorious'* first season with Canadian Maritime Union crews, after several seasons of being manned by Hal Banks' Seafarers' International Union Canadian District.

It started with strange phone calls at the St. Catharines, Ontario, home of John McNamara, lockmaster at Lock 1 of the Welland Canal and president of Local 212 of the CBRT. Sometimes there would be no one on the end of the line. Other times it was heavy breathing or insane laughter. There was never any conversation.

Often the calls were handled by his wife. When he worked from midnight to eight in the morning, most calls came in between about two and five in the morning. When he worked afternoons until midnight, she'd get the harassing calls between about nine-thirty and eleven at night. There were too many calls to keep an accurate estimate. On May 24, 1962, the day after his wedding anniversary, he got an unlisted number. Also that spring, someone slashed the tires of his car. Then a caterer showed up at his office with an expensive meal he hadn't ordered.

On June 8, 1962, McNamara sent a telegram to Prime Minister John Diefenbaker:

> Sir. Urge immediate enquiry into SIU tactics, finances, etc. As requested by Claude Jodoin in letter to you dated May 23, 1962.

Ottawa already knew more than enough about Hal Banks. By this point, the Conservatives had received two secret reports on Banks from the RCMP. The first, delivered by hand to Justice Minister E. Davie Fulton on February 23, 1959, included this warning by Commissioner L.H. Nicholson: "It seems clear to me that the report discloses a most unhealthy situation and one which warrants some further action." The thirty-three-page report noted that Banks had thrown thousands of sailors out of work by branding them communists. "It is inconceivable that the industry embraced that many persons of Communist sympathies," the report stated. "It is also improper that . . . any . . . individual has the power to arbitrarily label a man 'Communist' or to prohibit him from being employed at his normal occupation. This is the situation that exists today."

It further described irregularities in the handling of the union's $900,000 welfare fund. Also noted was the Seafarers' unusually high rate of turnover and Banks' affection for Jimmy Hoffa and Dave Beck of the International Teamsters. Finally, the report warned, "It is high probable that physical violence will be resorted to if found expedient."

A Department of Labour official wrote back to McNamara to say that the matter was receiving serious attention. Then, on the night of June 19, the matter became very personal to the men of Local 212. On the next day the local was to hold special meetings on the Great Lakes/St. Lawrence Seaway situation. There had been talk of a canal boycott and members were to decide if they'd back the CLC if it took retaliatory action. Every day that spring seemed to bring news of another beating. The common bond of victims was that they had openly opposed Hal Banks' Seafarers' International Union.

On the eve of the meeting, McNamara headed off to work at 11:30 p.m. He thought of how tired he'd be the next day when he was conducting two meetings after having worked all night. As he stepped out his back door, McNamara was clubbed across the head. He couldn't see how he was hit or who hit him. All he could see were four feet slamming into him. One man kept on kicking him while the other clubbed him in the head. He was conscious enough to shield his head with his arm and shout for help at the top of his voice.

When the attackers fled, McNamara could only think that he needed medical attention, but he didn't want to startle his wife. He made a vain attempt to crawl to his car to drive to the hospital. Realizing this was hopeless, he crawled back to his house and pulled himself up to the doorbell.

"My God, John, what happened to you?" his wife cried.

"I don't know. Someone has beaten me on the head. Would you call a doctor and phone the canal office that I'll not be coming in to work."

By this time, neighbours had rushed over. They dialed a doctor and the police, since Mrs. McNamara was too upset to dial a number. The police believed that McNamara had been clubbed with his own garden shears. The blows were strong enough to snap the handles away from the steel blades. It took thirty-two stitches to seal McNamara's forehead and another fourteen for a gash on the top of his head. Doctors told him he also had suffered a concussion and cerebral blood clot, a lacerated left ear and that the soft tissue and ligaments of his right arm were severely torn. Long after the cuts were healed, he would suffer from numbness on the right side of his head.

The next day, Local 212 passed a resolution strongly condemning the SIU action on the canals "as representing an unwarranted and illegal interference with the rights of Canadian sailors," and resolved to back the CMU fully in its war with the SIU.

The phone calls to the McNamaras continued. Now they were even more obscene and the worst of them were received by Mrs.

McNamara, already suffering from cystic fibrosis. McNamara wasn't able to work until July 17. A week later, the harassing calls to his home forced him to get a new unlisted number.

The Canadian Labour Congress had been pressuring Ottawa for a full-scale inquiry into Banks' activities. Jodoin had warned that someone might be killed if Banks wasn't brought under control. When nothing was done, CLC vice-president Bill Dodge began planning a boycott of the St. Lawrence Seaway. Traffic passing through the Seaway was worth more than $2,500,000,000 a year. If it stopped moving, the government would have to take notice.

The boycott began July 5, 1962. At a downtown Ottawa restaurant, Bill Dodge savoured lunch that day with his boycott committee, knowing that they had finally forced Ottawa to act. A call came to the restaurant, requesting Dodge to report to Labour minister Michael Starr as soon as possible. Dodge continued on with his meal at a leisurely pace, then went to Starr's office.

Starr greeted him with a good-natured curse.

"I could have obtained an injunction against you at eight-thirty this morning," he said.

"You could have got one at seven-thirty this morning," Dodge replied. "You and everyone else had known about the boycott for days."

Starr asked Dodge how long he would maintain the boycott. Dodge replied that it would continue until they had some indication from him that the federal government would meet some of their requests. The CLC wanted a complete investigation of Banks' administration, high-level efforts by Ottawa to end the boycotting of Canadian vessels in the U.S. and a program to prosecute those responsible for the past two years of waterfront bloodshed.

Starr was agreeable to the first two points. There would be an inquiry and there would be communication with the U.S. But a Department of Justice official present argued that the third proposal would interfere with provincial and municipal jurisdictions. Dodge replied that the CLC didn't want Ottawa to start criminal investigations within provincial jurisdictions. They just wanted federal authorities to offer to cooperate with other police forces.

As they argued, a call came in that the Seaway was now entirely blocked. The captain of the SIU-crewed *Blanche Hindman* had retaliated against the CLC by barricading the Welland Canal. Ironically, Hal Banks, the man sent to Canada to keep communists from tying up the St. Lawrence Seaway, had shut it down himself, something the communists had never accomplished.

The next day, Dodge received an injunction and the boycott was called off. The CLC had won its first major campaign in its war with Hal Banks. Hostilities would now shift from the waterfront to commission hearing rooms.

16

When I saw everything that I was uncovering in that place, I was a little bit worried.

Young lawyer Marc Lalonde comments on studying Seafarers' office records

The inquiry was to be headed by the imposing Thomas Grantham Norris, a B.C. admiralty judge with a tall, powerful build, silver hair and no-nonsense stare. Norris refused to suffer fools in his courtroom, cuffing them back into line with terse, blunt comments in a voice that rose ever so slightly under stress. Norris had few precedents to draw upon for what was to be the most extensive hearing of its kind ever held in Canada. Before him was a collection of singularly strong-willed adversaries, including a future Ontario Appeals Court judge, a future Canadian Finance minister and a future arms supplier for Muammar al-Qaddafi.

The inquiry began in Ottawa on August 7, 1962, and would rotate through Toronto, St. Catharines, Montreal and back to Ottawa during the 108 days that it sat. Its mandate was to examine shipping disruptions on the Great Lakes but it was soon painfully obvious that the real topics were Hal C. Banks and his code of violence. As his commission counsel, Norris chose Charles Dubin, a genteel, forty-year-old Toronto lawyer who had earned his stellar reputation by saving a dozen clients from the gallows and, at the age of only twenty-nine, became one of the youngest lawyers ever to be honoured with the designation of King's Council. His skill in cross-examination was so acute and his manner so pleasant that he could fillet a witness and leave him smiling.

Representing the CLC was Maurice Wright, a handsome veteran of labour wars who lived his morals and was armed with a withering sense of righteous indignation. Acting for Upper Lakes was Jack Geller, a Toronto lawyer specializing in commercial law. Beneath his disarming glibness, Geller fully realized the seriousness of the case: a thug had tried to break into his hotel room at three in the morning. Shortly after the hearings began, an anonymous caller threatened his wife on the phone.

For the commission, Banks reactivated John Ahern, once again his top lawyer, following the dismissal of John Schlesinger. But in the forefront was Joe Nuss, from the firm of Hyde and Ahern, and Toronto lawyer Bruce Thomas, both in their mid-twenties. Throughout the hearings, Banks would trot out enough lawyers to field a baseball squad, with alternates and cheerleaders. A few of the designated hitters included the Honourable R.L. Kellock, Q.C., former Supreme Court Justice, and Gordon F. Henderson, Q.C., former president of the Canadian Bar Association.

Wright and Geller wasted no time in setting the tone for the hearings, as dozens of victims of waterfront violence—including Alfred and Stella Scavanelli—were paraded before the commission. Norris listened to numbing accounts of women being attacked in their own homes and men being beaten into unconsciousness by strangers. He heard about victims who were afraid to leave their homes, let alone testify before the commission. Another assault victim with his arm in a cast told how a beating by a half-dozen men on a Montreal street had rendered him unfit for work. He wasn't afraid to tell his story, but refused to give his address, arguing, "I don't want my family to be bothered."

In the background was Jimmy Todd, making sure the victims were as presentable as possible. Todd kept a supply of freshly pressed white shirts. He passed them out to witnesses before they took the stand, then retrieved them as soon as their testimony had been recorded.

The commission played to packed courtrooms from its opening day, appealing to anyone interested in nationalism, the movement of Canadian wheat or a good story. People had heard about Banks' war with Upper Lakes Shipping and mainstream labour and they wanted to see the man who had shut down the Seaway. Curiosity seekers vied for good seats with a blend of union and shipping figures. With the proceedings for the duration were Arthur Bryden of *The Globe and Mail* and Robert Rice of Canadian Press, whose wire stories were run coast-to-coast.

"By the time the Norris Commission started, there was a great deal of public interest," Geller recalls. "It was a national issue."

Researching commission counsel Dubin's case were chartered accountant Alan G. Watson of Peat Marwick Mitchell & Co. in Toronto, and a relatively unknown young Montreal lawyer named Marc Lalonde. It was late in the first week of September that Banks offered to open his books to the commission. Lalonde and Watson were rushed in before he could change his mind.

The two refined gentlemen were unlikely fixtures in Banks' office for more than two months. Each day, they'd pass union goons like Jack Casper and Eldon Richardson on their way into the penthouse office. On one occasion, it was "Tough Tony" Anastasia of the International Longshoremen's Association who dropped by. (Anastasia's New York waterfront operation provided the basis for the film *On the Waterfront*. His brother, Albert "The Executioner," had also achieved notoriety—first for running the contract-killing group nicknamed "Murder Incorporated," and then as a mob boss. Perhaps he's best remembered for a photo taken of him in a barber chair in 1957, moments after he was shot to death.)

When Watson and Lalonde arrived, Banks would call them into his penthouse office for an audience. He would be sitting behind his kidney-shaped desk, his face framed by the bay windows with the magnificent view of the Montreal skyline and Mount Royal in the background. It was an imposing sight for Watson and Lalonde, who were seated on lowslung chairs that had them almost squatting on the floor. "Our behinds couldn't have been more than six inches from the floor," Watson recalled.

Banks was a cooperative host, and his office staff would bring the two investigators coffee even as they helped build the case against Banks. Lalonde would often wonder why Banks was so accommodating. Perhaps it was simply his arrogance—his belief that he was truly untouchable. On the other hand, perhaps he was simply flexing his muscle. He was Hal Banks. He didn't have to hide things. Perhaps he thought most of the damaging information in the SIU files had been destroyed. This possibility is supported by Harry Crowe, a researcher for the CBRT, who booked a hotel room across the street so that he could spy into the Seafarers' hall. The weekend before Lalonde and Watson arrived, Crowe observed people in the room holding the records working well into the night. When Lalonde and Watson arrived, they found that several of Banks' files were empty.

What they did discover, however, was a pile of reports on 8 1/2''-by-11'' forms, with the headings ''Do Not Ship'' and ''Report of Charges.'' But when Lalonde later tried to obtain them, they had vanished. Lalonde also discovered a motorized index filing system for sailors' union cards, which included a section called ''Not in Order.'' Lalonde counted the names of 3,399 sailors banned from sailing. Some were accused of jumping ship when it came time to pay their dues, others were accused of habitual drunkenness, drug addiction and sexual perversion. Lalonde decided to list only the most flagrant examples of abuses of power; his list contained 1,200 names.

The investigation of the SIU books turned up a dichotomy which mirrored Banks' handling of the union. Controls on office staff and sailors were tight, but for Banks they appeared nonexistent. Of more than $80,000 that he charged to expenses between 1959 and 1962, vouchers were only provided for $8,220. Banks travelled with blank cheques, presigned by the union's co-signing officer, which he used to draw from union funds, apparently at will.

Expensive home repairs, bills from Tony the Tailor and a woman's fur coat were also charged to the union. So were the white Cadillacs he bought each year and his expensive powerboat. All were registered in Banks' name. Even his cigarettes were billed to the union. When he stayed at hotels, they were only the best, like the Waldorf Astoria or the Hotel de La Concha in Puerto Rico, where he ran up a $3,661 bill. Nor was the then-single Banks lonely in his costly digs: the hotel registers were often signed ''Mr. and Mrs. Banks.'' Watson and Lalonde also found that union money was used to fund flights for his nurse-girlfriend and his father.

Other expenses also raised eyebrows. The names of a half-dozen Montreal Liberal campaign officials for the June 1962 election were listed as receiving contributions of $500 each. A former Seafarers' bookkeeper told of regular payments to a Montreal *Gazette* reporter. The books contained a note explaining $1,001 went to "detective fees paid out of Union funds re to keep eye on Droeger Drew and the boys." The reference dated back to 1954, when sailor John Droeger and Opposition Leader George Drew fought Banks' trip to the International Labour Organization in Geneva. Watson and Lalonde also noted that a payment of $1,000 had been made to a Montreal policeman shortly after he sang Banks' praises to the citizenship judge at his hearing in 1958.

Watson and Lalonde found evidence of U.S. bank accounts, which fitted in with the story told by one of Banks' former lovers, who said he was squirreling money away in the U.S. for the day that he would return. But since the powers of an industrial inquiry commission weren't as far-reaching as those of a royal commission, they weren't able to subpoena the U.S. accounts and trace what transactions had gone through them.

Much of Watson's and Lalonde's information came from a former SIU bookkeeper, driven out by nerves that were frayed after four years of working for Banks. She described what it was like to be given the job of training an assistant whose only qualifications for the job had been fondled by a city-hall official who was close to Banks. Soon after she arrived, money mysteriously went missing from Seafarers' funds. The bookkeeper then had threatened to quit over her nubile assistant, whom she considered dishonest and incompetent. "You do that and I'll say that you took the money and you will never earn your living again," Banks warned.

She would later find that leaving the union hall didn't mean escaping Banks. She had lined up a job with Quality Press and was to begin work on Monday, December 5, 1960. The Thursday before she was to start, she got a phone call from her new boss. He said he had just spoken to Banks, then asked if she thought Banks would really stop doing business with Quality Press if she were hired. The next day, she got another phone call from Quality Press telling her she had lost the job.

Banks' SIU records ''made pretty awful reading once in a while,'' Lalonde said. ''But what's amazing is that they didn't mind putting it on the record there. When I saw everything that I was uncovering in that place, I was a little bit worried . . . But Alan Watson was with me. We were always in the building more or less at the same time and Alan had all the information that I had. So, had they bounced me out they would still have to bump Alan. I was there for two months at least and I never was threatened . . . Quite often I would go up to see Hal Banks in his penthouse over there and ask him for comments on information about this or that. And he would receive me, be very charming, and he was pretty straightforward. He had quite clearly the ethics of a certain milieu that you do not hesitate to be rough with your own people but you don't touch the police or the lawyers. . . .''

Frank Drea, then labour writer for the Toronto *Telegram,* recalled there was a feeling that Lalonde was in danger. At a strange meeting with Justice Norris and Charles Dubin, Drea describes that they got word that Lalonde was going to be attacked

> . . . We were in Ottawa, while the hearings were on in Ottawa in one of the crucial stages . . . Mr. Justice Norris and Mr. Justice Dubin (Dubin later became an Ontario Appeals Court judge) asked me to see them one day. They explained to me that they were in receipt of information that Mr. Lalonde . . . would be in some personal danger. They had information that Banks' people in Quebec had decided to make an example out of Mr. Lalonde . . . Mr. Lalonde at that time was not a Liberal . . . They couldn't get at Mr. Dubin and they couldn't get at Mr. Norris. But Mr. Lalonde was causing them a great deal of difficulty with the work that he was doing in Quebec. The thing was put to me, would I be Mr. Lalonde's bodyguard?''

The idea was that the powerfully built Drea would be less obtrusive than a police guard. Drea agreed. But instead of having to brawl, the rumpled reporter was given a lesson in culture. ''Mr.

Lalonde's a very fine man,'' Drea recalled of his time with the Oxford-educated young lawyer. ''Mr. Lalonde taught me about art. Mr. Lalonde is not the type of man who sat around drinking beer. He taught me all about Riopelle . . . . [We went] over to the National Gallery and nothing ever happened and Mr. Lalonde went on to better things.''

Leading the union probe into Banks' activities was Harry Sherman Crowe, research director for the CBRT. Crowe had the ability to maintain an air of innocence and invincibility amidst chaos as he ferreted out information for Maurice Wright's case. Crowe's young assistant Ivan Timonim joked that if Crowe were attacked by someone waving a knife, Crowe would have immediately begun advising his attacker on how to clean rust from his knife blade. Through sheer innocence or guile—or a magical combination of both—Crowe would be able to slide out of the situation, perhaps even making a friend in the process.

Crowe wasn't afraid to interview anyone, including Banks himself. Recalling Crowe's description of his trip to Banks' Point Claire home, CBRT secretary-treasurer Don Secord says that, ''While he was there, a cat walked into the room and Banks picked up the cat and set it on the mantel and pulled out a gun and shot the cat. . . . He petted the cat first . . . I think it was meant to impress [Crowe].''

Banks had badly miscalculated in trying to scare Crowe. The stocky little academic had the zeal of a crusader and seemed able to blank fear out of his mind. It was natural for Crowe to funnel his entire being towards a definable, righteous goal. So, if anything, Banks just reinforced what Crowe had already suspected. Crowe had heard stories of men who had run and had their legs broken or had been thrown through windows. One former Seafarers' worker told of how outspoken Toronto SIU patrolman Ray Power was believed to have been murdered on the highway in the summer of 1959. The informant added that Banks forbade one of Power's friends to attend the funeral. Another informant told Crowe that the wife of a union man was raped in front of her husband in Banks' office. There were many others, but not all the people telling these horror stories shared Crowe's zeal in getting the truth. One informant threatened to commit suicide if called before the Norris Commission. Another left on a long holiday to the U.S. after being approached by Crowe.

Crowe was willing to interview anyone who might help the case against Banks. He drafted a list of twenty-two women who had been Banks' lovers in 1957, hoping that the spurned playmates might help topple the waterfront warlord. But one woman connected with the Seafarers almost tricked Crowe into a rendezvous with SIU goons. Crowe and an assistant had made contact through a third party with a woman who worked for the SIU. They were told that she was sick of Banks and ready to help Crowe. Working through the third party, she agreed to an interview in a room at the Windsor Hotel in Montreal. Crowe arrived first and as he was setting up his tape recorder, his assistant glanced out the window and down onto the street and screamed "My God! See the woman out there and the man who's with her?" The man was one of Banks' goons. Crowe realized they had been set up. They scrambled down the back stairs to their car and raced for the Ontario border.

"They were just driving as quickly as they could, hoping they'd be stopped by a policeman," Canadian Labour Congress lawyer Maurice Wright recalls, "but they weren't even sure about that, because they were afraid the police were in cahoots with the SIU. So they were heading straight for Ottawa to get out of the Quebec jurisdiction."

Around eleven that night, Crowe called Wright, asking him to arrange police protection. Wright called a deputy minister of labour. "We had a row," Wright remembers. ". . . He was just too busy. He didn't believe me. . . . He said he could never get the RCMP to do anything now, at this hour of the night. And who would believe the story anyway? Why didn't we get in touch with the QPP—the Quebec Provincial Police? I said, 'Oh God . . . you just don't understand what this case is all about. We don't dare go to those police. How do we know they're not in cahoots with Banks?' " Wright called Crowe a few minutes later and said, "You're on your own. I can't get the guy to get off his butt."

''Okay,'' Crowe replied. ''Just hope for the best. I think we've lost them.''

Around one-thirty in the morning, Wright got another call. It was Crowe telling him they had made it back to Ontario alive.

A month into the hearings, Norris was making no effort to conceal his disgust. ''Without at all at this time deciding who is responsible for these attacks, these cowardly attacks, it is very difficult for me to understand how in this state of our so-called civilization, things of this sort could happen in Canada,'' Norris said. ''We have heard, day after day, witnesses coming here and telling us of the most cowardly attacks. That is why I referred to them as a pack of jackals.''

The hearings had begun in August; by September, Brooklyn-based Seafarers' International president Paul Hall could see that Banks needed help. Hall didn't have Banks' flair, but he could be counted on to get results. This was reflected in their organizations as well as their personalities. A joke at the Brooklyn Seafarers' hall was that Hall had secretaries who occasionally whored around while Banks hired whores who could type. Hall quickly assembled a talent pool and headed north to avert possible disaster.

17

Some guys really believe their own bullshit. You know what I mean? Banks was the kind of guy who believed his own crap.

Former CIA agent Edwin Wilson assesses Hal Banks

Eddie Mackin was in a bind. He had planned on being in Peru helping poor workers organize, not in Canada helping a petty tyrant like Banks cling to power. But a revolt in Peru had spoiled the young union official's plans for working in South America. Now, suddenly, Paul Hall had him on a witness stand in Montreal. Mackin's task was clear-cut and impossible: he was to make the Canadian District of the SIU look democratic.

It was obvious why Hall wanted Mackin. He was personable, honest, newly married, university-educated and likeable. That Mackin had no criminal record was another definite asset—and a unique one among the SIU officials who were called upon to defend Banks. Also making him a good witness was the fact that he hadn't even met Banks until that autumn. It was easier to vouch for Banks' organization when you weren't fully familiar with it.

Mackin had come to the SIU from the Retail Clerks' Union, which routinely swapped muscle for brains with the Seafarers. He was in Montreal because of his respect for Paul Hall, not Hal Banks, but it didn't take long for him to realize that Banks was unique. Shortly after arriving in town, Mackin had asked a SIU secretary in the union-hall lobby if she could recommend a restaurant in the neighbourhood. Banks boomed in on the intercom, ''Leave that girl alone!'' Not untypically, he had been monitoring their conversation from his sixth-floor office. Later, Mackin would witness yet another demonstration of how Banks loved to play with the buttons by his desk. The morning after a midnight tryst with Banks, one of Paul Hall's officeworkers called his office. With a collection of union officials, including Mackin, in the room with him, Banks switched on the intercom so that all the boys could listen to the lovestruck woman rhapsodizing about the evening before, completely unaware of her audience.

There was a general feeling among Paul Hall's men that Banks had been invited up to Canada to fight the communists. Having done this, the government was turning around and trying to throw him out. Perhaps Banks wasn't perfect, but he wasn't being fairly treated. The Hall men weren't about to desert one of their own. Mackin says Hall saw Banks' problems as a stumbling block in Hall's ambitions to move up the AFL-CIO, of which the SIU was a member.

The SIU situation was as intense as it was bizarre. Mackin was called on to prepare for a day's proceedings at the hearings, go to the hearings, do a post-mortem of the current day and then prepare for the next day. He helped draw up a series of charts and figures aimed at making the Canadian District appear to be benefiting its members.

When Mackin took the stand, he thought it would be just a matter of hours. It lasted days and the grilling was intense. Hall would later say that it destroyed Eddie Mackin. And almost a quarter-century later, it still hurts Mackin to talk about it. "I was playing a role without having preread the script," he says. "I didn't know there was a script. I was not prepared to play the role in which I was cast."

It was obvious that Eddie Mackin had been hung out to dry. Instead of just presenting the SIU's carefully crafted figures, Mackin found himself under personal attack. His post-secondary education was belittled by opposition counsel Maurice Wright. Edwin Wilson, another international representative, recalls that Hall was livid.

"That night, I'll never forget that night as long as I live," Wilson recalls. "About eleven o'clock at night and we're in the middle of this fucking union hall and Hall is screaming at this sonofabitch, 'Mackie, you stupid shit! When you get up there, I don't want you to do anything! Just keep your mouth shut!' The next day, Mackie goes up there and says all this shit again. He'd go up there and say all this crap again. You know, finally after about six days on the stand, newspapers are eating him alive.

''Paul takes him into the room and he says, very quietly, 'Listen.' He took out a three-by-five card and he wrote on it, I d-o-n-'t k-n-o-w. And he said, 'If you say anything on the stand other than, I d-o-n-'t k-n-o-w, I'm going to kill you.'

''So, Mackie went up there and they said, 'What's your name?'

'' 'I d-o-n-'t k-n-o-w.' ''

''This goddam King's Counsel was going bananas. And he said to him, 'Were you ever in the SIU?'

'' 'I d-o-n-'t k-n-o-w.' ''

''So they put it in the newspapers. 'The I Don't Know Boy.' ''

Mackin had no personal knowledge of any criminal activity in the SIU except for the Do Not Ship list, which was now called ''the Report of Charges.'' He dreaded being asked about it. And when he was, he denied knowing of the list's existence, although not without first trying to dodge the question. But Wright was unrelenting.

WRIGHT: Please answer my question, and we are wasting an awful lot of time. My question to you is: did you see anything in the minutes of any men during the two-and-a-half year period who had been placed on the DNS list? And you know what I am talking about.
MACKIN: DNS?
WRIGHT: Yes.
THE COMMISSIONER: Don't suggest you don't know what DNS means.
WRIGHT: Maybe you don't.
THE COMMISSIONER: Do you know what it means?
MACKIN: Yes, my lord.
THE COMMISSIONER: Well, then, all right. Why exhibit such a surprised expression?
WRIGHT: Did you see any men who had been placed on the DNS list?
MACKIN: No. I saw no record of men being placed on the DNS list.
WRIGHT: Now, we are talking about democracy in action. I

want your opinion. Were any men placed on DNS or on ROC or on . . .
THE COMMISSIONER: Explain that.
WRIGHT: You know what I mean by ROC, do you not?
MACKIN: No.
WRIGHT: Report of Charges. Do you know what I am talking about when I talk of Report of Charges?
MACKIN: No.
WRIGHT: Do you not have a Report of Charges in the SIU of North America?
MACKIN: I don't know.
WRIGHT: Did you ever have, or hear of a DNS in the SIU of North America? Yes or no?
MACKIN: In the . . .
WRIGHT: Yes or no.
MACKIN: No.

The experience on the stand would haunt Mackin for years.

Edwin Wilson, who had also been brought to Montreal by Hall as an international representative, was spared the ordeal of giving testimony. But it would have been fascinating if he had been called to the stand. Tall, violent and vulgar, Wilson was working for the Central Intelligence Agency as a secret agent at the same time that he worked for Hall's U.S. Seafarers. Wilson says he never told Hall about his CIA affiliation. And while Wilson is a proven and well-practised liar, the statement is probably true. The records of author Peter Maas, whose book *Manhunt* is about Wilson's life in the CIA, indicate that Hall did not know Wilson was also a CIA agent in the summer of 1962.

But Eddie Mackin recalls a curious conversation with SIU official Morris Weisberger around 1980, when Wilson's double life was becoming public knowledge. "He told me that Paul Hall came by in 1960 or 1961," Mackin recalls, "and asked Morris to give him a union book. Morris said that as a president he was authorized to grant him a full book, something that now takes from five to ten years of shipping to earn because it's practically closed to outsiders.'' In fact, there was no evidence of Wilson having paid dues to the union in any of the three places dues payments are recorded.

One has to wonder exactly what Wilson was doing in Canada. As he tells the story, he was pushed to the limit preparing Banks' case. But most of the key SIU representatives interviewed can't even remember Wilson being there. Mackin remembers Wilson coming north for the Norris Commission, but he said he can't remember Wilson doing any work.

Months after the commission debacle, Mackin would quit the SIU. Five years later, he would read in Jack Anderson's syndicated muckraking column that his year on full scholarship at the labour school of Cornell had been financed by the CIA. A decade and a half later, he'd have an odd feeling when he saw Ed Wilson's picture on the evening news. Wilson, another graduate of the Cornell Labour School, had double-crossed the CIA and was running weapons for Muammar al-Qaddafi. Wilson, who had long ago left the union, was accused of trying to feed atomic-weapons secrets to the Libyan dictator and convicted of placing murder contracts on ten of his own enemies. Although his salary had never exceeded $32,000 a year, he had a fortune of more than $15 million and his Virginia neighbours included Elizabeth Taylor and her then-husband Senator John Warner, as well as tycoon Jack Kent Cooke, owner of the Washington Redskins of the National Football League.

Wilson's neighbourhood has changed somewhat, as he now lists his address as the federal penitentiary in Marion, Illinois. This institution has replaced Alcatraz as the toughest prison in the United States, and Wilson's fellow prisoners include gangs like the Aryan Brotherhood and the Mexican Mafia. It's a prison safe from escapes and break-ins. Aside from double walls topped with razor wire, the prison is armed with surface-to-air missiles, lest any gang members on the outside attempt an air strike to rescue their friends. Wilson is housed in K wing, away from the general population who might use his anti-American activities as an excuse to kill him.

Wilson's memories of Banks could serve as a commentary on his own life. "Some guys really believe their own bullshit," he said recently in an interview. "You know what I mean? Banks was the kind of guy who believed his own crap."

18

To me personally, anything over a $100 bill is a big sum of money.

Hal Banks declares himself a penurious man

By the time Banks was called to the stand at the Norris Commission for a lengthy testimony in early January 1963, the public wondered what sort of monster he was. Previous witnesses had described rivals being beaten in front of their families. There seemed to be no end to stories of contract brutality and gross abuses of union funds. Now, after four months of hearing others talk about Hal Banks, there was finally the chance to hear the man himself.

Banks loved it. He cherished the spotlight, even if it illuminated things he would rather keep in the dark. During his eight days on the stand, the two sides of his personality waged a war against each other in the normally sombre Exchequer Court in Ottawa. At times, he displayed a paranoid's obsession with secrecy, refusing to admit that any violence or any blacklisting even existed, despite overwhelming evidence to the contrary. At other times, he all but dared the commission to do something about his financial excesses, perhaps knowing many members of the rank-and-file lived vicariously through his spending.

His testimony began with an unctuous show of respect for commission counsel Charles Dubin, praising his fairness. Dubin had qualities to which Banks aspired. He had real power and didn't need a baseball bat to make a point. Dubin gently took hold of Banks' ego and led him into traps. Banks seemed to enjoy the journey, if not the destination, as Dubin let him describe himself as a spendthrift.

DUBIN: Do you not agree with me that in spending the money of a union that there is a high degree of responsibility and trust in any officer of the union?
BANKS: Oh, absolutely.
DUBIN: And that money should be expended . . .
BANKS: Judiciously.
DUBIN: . . . judiciously to advance the cause of the union?
BANKS: Every penny.

Banks went on to tell Dubin that, ''To me personally, anything over a $100 bill is a big sum of money.'' He explained that the SIU executive had wanted to pay him $50,000 a year, but he refused to accept a penny over $20,000.

Banks had always prided himself on his vocabulary, although one could argue that he bludgeoned the language as brutally as he did his waterfront opponents. Each Monday morning, he would gather SIU officials at his home to map out the union's goals for the upcoming week. Part of the Monday-morning ritual included Banks marching to a dictionary mounted prominently on a lectern on his main floor. He'd choose what he considered an impressive word that he wanted to add to his vocabulary. Then for the next week he'd use the word continually, exploring all its possibilities until the next Monday, when the cycle would be repeated with a new set of polysyllables.

Banks' time on the stand gave him a chance to show off the results of the word exercises that had irritated and amused his SIU executive. When Dubin sought a word to describe Banks' scrutiny of union finances, Banks proudly offered ''penurious.''

''I have worked twenty hours a day since 1949 on this Canadian situation,'' he said. ''There is no question about that.'' Moreover, Banks continued, his sole holiday amidst this selfless struggle was a brief respite after his mentor Harry Lundeberg died in 1957. And when pressed about his 1960 spring sojourn in Puerto Rico, Banks explained that the sun and surf couldn't stop him from working twenty hours a day. Asked if this could be considered a holiday, Banks was indignant: ''I should say not.''

Neither did he see any fiscal irresponsibility in his decision to ship his Eldorado down to Puerto Rico rather than rent a foreign compact. He told Dubin that this had been done with his own funds, even though it had been used for union business, including driving in three parades.

Dubin had struck a rich vein in allowing Banks to speak of his Cadillac. Forgotten were Banks' previous declarations of ''penuriousness.'' He explained that he came to save Canada behind the wheel of a Cadillac, and wasn't about to lower his standards. He was in the habit of buying a new one each year. The union would pick up the difference between the trade-in and cost of a new one. In fact, his current car was eleven months old and due to be replaced shortly. With that Dubin presented Banks with a bill from February 27, 1959:

> DUBIN: I suggest to you that was to produce a shiny new Cadillac?
> BANKS: Yes, a big, long one.
> DUBIN: A long one?
> BANKS: Yes.
> DUBIN: And then February 17, 1960?
> BANKS: A white Cadillac, Mr. Dubin.

Dubin pursued his personal attack.

> DUBIN: Do you like looking at yourself all the time?
> BANKS: No I do not.
> DUBIN: What do you need 14 mirrors in an apartment for?
> BANKS: Well, there was a need for them. That is a part of the decoration of the apartment. That is a question of judgment, Mr. Dubin.

Dubin then decided to question Banks' judgment in spending $15,000 to furnish the luxury apartment, including $1,082 for the mirrors. The apartment, complete with maid service, was in addition to his penthouse atop the St. James Street office and his Pointe Claire waterfront home.

''I notice here a sofa for $1,180,'' he said. ''Isn't that quite a bit of money for a sofa?''

''Well, it is quite a bit of money for anything, but furniture is expensive, Mr. Dubin. If you have bought any furniture recently you know that. You do not get any kind of furniture for nothing."

"Do you agree that one sofa at $1,180 is an expensive sofa?"

"I would not say that. I can show you sofas that cost $5,000 and $6,000. This was not a custom piece either, it was a stock piece of furniture."

Banks bristled when questioned about his spending, particularly concerning entertainment. "When you use the word 'entertainment' you seem to raise your voice a little," he chastised Dubin. A five-day convention in 1959 cost the union $24,000, including $5,000 that went to the El Morocco night club, in which Banks had shares. "I got dollar for dollar value," he said. ". . . These things just don't happen, Mr. Dubin. It is very necessary for us to keep up relationships and to keep up appearances, and keep up many other things. Now, I would say this, that if it cost twenty-five times as much as it shows in those accounts to maintain that, and if it is worth the money, then I do not think it is misused or not, shall we say, unjudiciously used." Banks said he could give the audit committee exact explanations of where money went, should they ask.

"Are you serious?" Dubin asked.

"I have to be," Banks replied.

Banks was less flippant when the questions turned to union violence. He acted baffled that it should even be mentioned. He drew a blank when asked about the beating of Captain Walsh, described earlier by Michael Sheehan, Richard Greaves and Walsh himself. Banks said he hadn't even heard of it, let alone been its author. Big Jack Casper, who had nearly beaten Walsh to death, was described by Banks as an "international representative" who "helped us from time to time." Casper currently "mothers" SIU witnesses for the commission hearings, Banks continued. "And furthermore I do not operate on that level. I have been in the union business too long to operate on that level."

"What do you mean, 'that level'?" Dubin asked.

"On the level of violence."

Banks flatly denied any knowledge that systematic violence existed, let alone could be traced to his union. Pressed for some kind of explanation for the mayhem, Banks suggested that private detectives were responsible for at least one of the beatings. But Justice Norris pressed the point.

NORRIS: All counsel is asking you is do you know that this violence existed?
BANKS: I do not know that it existed. I have not seen one single case of it. I have not heard of any conviction in regard to it.
NORRIS: Never mind convictions.
BANKS: You said counsel wanted to know if I knew anything about it.
NORRIS: You say no.
BANKS: I say no.

But for all of Banks' protestations of innocence, there was a thinly veiled warning to dissidents who might be inspired by the commission. Any man in his union has recourse to the courts of Canada for justice, Banks stated. As proof, he offered the example of John Droeger, the man who had disappeared and was widely assumed by the waterfront community to have been executed at Banks' command eight years earlier. Anyone who had heard the rumours about Droeger's fate couldn't have missed the message.

Any amicability that had existed between counsel and Banks during Dubin's examination quickly evaporated when Canadian Labour Congress lawyer Maurice Wright took over. Banks had approached Wright early in the inquiry and had heaped extravagant praise upon him. Wright saw this as a ploy and kept his distance. Icy, sarcastic and experienced, Wright baited Banks when he finally faced him on the stand.

WRIGHT: Is it credible to you that in our society—this Canadian society of ours—that over a three-year period not a single proposition that you have placed before your membership has ever been opposed by your members?
BANKS: Is it credulous?
WRIGHT: Take your choice, credible or credulous.

BANKS: Which word did you use?
WRIGHT: I said "credible." Is it believable?
BANKS: All right. The question is, is it believable.
WRIGHT: Yes.
BANKS: It certainly is. It is the fact.
WRIGHT: Is it reasonable?
BANKS: It is reasonable. It is the fact.

Wright went on to note that Banks, the self-described penurious leader, charged his drycleaning, toothbrushes and even kitty litter to the union.

Now the man who had dreamed of leading all Canada's unionized workers—and perhaps even all Canadians—was reduced to trying to dodge pointed questions about kitty litter. "I have a cat at my house, yes," he said. "This particular cat sand was for the building. They put the cat sand down there. My cat don't need sand, he gets outdoors, but you can't let a cat out on St. James Street or he will be hit with a car."

When Wright shifted his sights to the Do Not Ship list, Banks replied that there was no DNS list anymore, that it had been discontinued after the 1954 Droeger case. Then Wright proceeded to unravel list upon list of blacklisted sailors, constantly noting Banks' signature on each one.

Wright produced a name from the union files dated July 30, 1956, with a note beside a sailor's name which read, "Recommend that his book stay in retirement for ever and ever, amen." Banks said this didn't prove the man was blacklisted. It just proved his union had a sense of humour.

Harry Crowe, the man who had uncovered the lists, sat in the back of the courtroom, his hangdog expression belying his enjoyment of the spectacle as Wright pressed on with his calculated dissection. Banks' credibility was shot, his denials proving as damning as his admissions. The work of Watson, Lalonde and Crowe had paid off magnificently.

The night before they got Banks on the stand, Crowe and Wright discussed Banks' personality, setting traps to appeal to what they considered his weaknesses. As Wright recalls, "He just fell into every bloody trap we sprung. We couldn't believe it."

Claude Jodoin of the CLC must have known the question was coming but there was no way to prepare for it. How could he defend his decision to back Banks in his 1957 citizenship application? Jodoin had said Hal Banks was a man of good character and "un actif pour le Canada."

"Il n'a pas manqué à l'etiquette," Jodoin had continued, meaning Banks didn't lack in morals or manners.

"That is very, high high applause for this man," Dubin reminded him. "I do not think you could say anything better about him."

"That's right," Jodoin replied. His voice was wistful, a cry from the heart of a man who knew he had made an enormous blunder. He took a pathetic stab at a joke, adding, "That is why I told you that when I make errors, I make some good ones."

Banks' opinion of Claude Jodoin had undergone a radical transformation since the 1950s, when he had praised him as a fellow battler against rapacious communist unions. Now Jodoin was a "fellow traveller," Banks charged. Paul Hall was even more blunt, calling Jodoin a whore.

Banks' political confusion showed up on the witness stand before the Norris Commission, where he accused Jodoin's CBRT associates of the mindboggling double heresy of being both communist- and company-controlled. Throwing in one more ideological full-gainer, Banks charged that feuding CBRT communists were to blame for the pummelling of Dick Greaves in Vancouver.

Banks' comments on international politics were even more tangled. He told the Norris Commission that a Cuban invasion of Canada would be a good thing for the SIU. Banks explained that he told his men in 1960 that Fidel Castro was preparing an invasion of Canada to take over strikebound CNS ships in Halifax. The ships were targeted for runs between the Soviet Union and Cuba, Banks claimed. This would help his rank-and-file by forcing Canada to end her neutrality in the U.S.–Cuba dispute.

''You seriously gave the impression, or your intent was to give the impression, that Cuban soldiers were coming into Canada to get these CNS ships?'' asked Wright, appearing dazed by the scenario.

''Well, Cuban soldiers did come into Canada to take them out at one time,'' Banks replied. The anti-communist crusader then said he offered to crew Castro's ships if Cuba posted a $1,400,000 bond, paid Canadian wage rates and kept the Canadian flag.

> WRIGHT: . . . Mr. Banks, are you an expert on communism?
> BANKS: Well, I know quite a bit about commies. I have been fighting them for a long time, Mr. Wright—successfully.
> WRIGHT: Successfully?
> BANKS: That's correct.
> NORRIS: Sometimes, Mr. Banks, it isn't a good thing, you know, to let the ghosts of the past haunt you too much. You just said that you had been fighting the communists. You were fighting the communists in the Canadian Seamen's Union days, that is what you say, and as I understand it your war-cry at that time was that they were communists. Is it not possible that the ghosts from the past are still haunting you?
> BANKS: No, it isn't, Mr. Commissioner. We are fighting them right today on the west coast. I don't think there is any secret about that.

Paul Hall could see that the Norris Commission was a no-win situation. SIU witnesses were uniformly unconvincing and chief lawyer Joe Nuss was treated by Norris as little more than an irritating schoolboy. ''He [Hall] wrote off Mr. Justice Norris and the whole commission of inquiry not long after he got there,'' SIU lawyer Bruce Thomas recalls, ''. . . this was what he called Georgia Justice. Georgia Justice is where they take you out and lynch you.''

Hall shifted his attack to the commission itself. The AFL-CIO Maritime Trades Department which he headed suddenly switched its annual convention from Hawaii to Montreal. And while Bill Dodge of the CLC was undergoing a lengthy cross-examination in a gloomy second-floor Montreal courtroom, Hall's conventioneers at the Mount Royal Hotel passed a resolution damning Dodge's conduct as ''inimical to all trade unions.'' While Dodge was being labelled a scab by the MTD, Banks was simultaneously being presented with a plaque for his union work. Suspicions were that Dodge was deliberately held on the stand so that his testimony would coincide with the convention.

Dodge was furious. And his testimony regarding Banks' violence fairly dripped with bitterness and sarcasm. ''One has to make one's decision about who is responsible by a process of elimination,'' Dodge said. ''In the army we used to refer to self-inflicted wounds. I don't think that we can consider that a possibility—that, for instance, an individual would take a crowbar and beat himself across the kneecap as a simple act of self-indulgence. I think the next possibility . . . is that the employees of the Upper Lakes Shipping company and members of the CMU are simply accident prone. . . . I think we have certainly to eliminate that. Obviously, there is a systematized program of beatings going on. If that is so, who is responsible for it? The Imperial Order of the Daughters of the Empire [*sic*]? The Women's Christian Temperance Union? The Steelworkers' Union? . . . The Seafarers' International Union is clearly responsible.''

Meanwhile, a group of SIU members had carried a coffin to Montreal's old courthouse, where the hearings were sitting. On it was a note which read, ''Here lies justice, buried by Norris.'' Then they marched into the courthouse's lobby and began handling out pamphlets entitled ''The Strange Conspiracy,'' which attempted to tie Upper Lakes Shipping with the CLC in a conspiracy to destroy the SIU of Canada, and hence ''to destroy the standards and security of Canadian workers.'' They went on in an attempt to establish a fictitious link between Upper Lakes Shipping and Chicago's boxing rackets and mobsters Blinky Palermo and Frankie Carbo.

Lawyer Bruce Thomas recalls that Justice Norris was furious. ''That's when the justice called me up . . . only Joe [Nuss] and I were acting for the union that day—and he laid it on the line. As

I recall, he said, 'Who's responsible for this? And you get this coffin out of the front and get rid of these pamphlets. And if I see it again, I'll hold you in contempt . . . .'

"That was the last straw, as I recall . . . I think I was tired of the shenanigans and it seemed to me it was just downhill from there. I just told the union, Look, if you need me, call me in Toronto for anything that I know about. You've got adequate representation. . . ."

Maurice Wright knew that he had the evidence to destroy Hal Banks. And it is probable that he would have used it, had it not been for a conversation between Wright and Norris that fall in Norris' chambers. As Wright recalls:

> Norris called me into chambers, into his own private office and he said, "You don't have to tell me this if you don't want to, but I've heard rumours to the effect that you might be leading evidence about Banks' involvement with certain Liberal politicians." When I said, "I have the evidence," he said, "I don't want to know what you've got. But listen to what an old man who has been through the mill has to say and then make your own decision and decide whatever you want to do. If you bring in evidence about Liberal politicians being friendly with Hal Banks, the Liberal party will then intervene in the inquiry and they will ask to be represented and what started out as an inquiry into shipping in Canada will be transformed by the politicians into a political event and the value of this inquiry will be shot down in flames."
>
> I hadn't thought of it that way and it made me think. I decided that he was right and I didn't put any of that evidence in. He had a certain prescience about him. He said, "You realize that originally I was a Tory. I was appointed by Diefenbaker. Diefenbaker was then in power . . . Remember that they were voted out in 1963." He said, "I don't know how long this inquiry is going to last but it's going to last longer than either of us imagined. When it's over, for all I

know, I may be reporting to a Liberal administration and not to a Conservative government.''

And that's entirely what happened. . . . He was absolutely right when he said to think twice before we put in political evidence. . . . We had to keep our eye on the ball. The important thing was to clean up the shipping mess and not get deflected into side issues.

19

This is not the time for anybody to have cold feet.

Former Banks ally Frank Hall describes the need for action against Hal Banks

Accountant Alan Watson received a telephone call from Justice Norris early in the winter of 1963. The hearings were over, and Justice Norris was working twelve-hour days drafting his report. He called to ask for clarification of a financial point. Somewhere towards the end of the conversation, Norris mentioned that he was lonely. The hearings hadn't been expected to last long, and secretaries had only been booked for a month. Norris' wife had stayed at their Pitt Meadows, B.C., home during the inquiry. Watson volunteered to come to Ottawa to help out. "By all means help," Norris replied.

Apparently, a rivalry had developed between Norris and Dubin during the inquiry, which contributed to Norris' solitude once the hearings ended. "It was rather amusing," Marc Lalonde remembers. "A kind of rivalry that developed between the two. Charlie Dubin would work on a cross-examination, et cetera, and prepare . . . or we would get some hot information and Charlie was obviously getting ready to get it [to] explode at the commission. And just as it was getting to the hot point, the judge would take over the cross-examination and get away with the headlines . . . . In the end, Dubin more or less didn't bother—left the commission for all practical purposes. He didn't put much time [in] once the cross-examinations were over. . . . Poor Judge Norris ended up being pretty well alone to finish the whole damn thing."

Watson found that Norris had a sense of the ridiculous, a useful defence mechanism when dealing with the subject of Hal Banks. At times, the austere judge seemed almost giddy. He entitled a report on Banks' associates as the "Rogues Gallery." When Watson presented him with a rough draft of a section of the report dealing with accounting, Norris replied: "Thank you very much. Now I'll put the swear words in."

"What do you mean by that?"

"Oh, I'll just make it a little livelier," Norris explained.

"Oh, can't I put them in to start with?"

"Oh, please do."

Norris was pushing himself hard and expected effort from others. At one point, he and Watson discussed writing shipping companies for statistics. "They may not choose to provide it," Watson cautioned. Leaving no doubt that he was serious, Norris replied, that if they didn't he would reconvene the hearings and require them to do it.

Norris didn't underestimate Banks' deviousness. But he did have a healthy respect for Banks' connections, having moved the commission from Montreal to Ottawa in the fall after hearing shadowy rumblings that moves were afoot to derail the Montreal hearings. Norris had also received warnings that his own life might be in danger. So, as Watson recalls, "he summarized the conclusions that he had arrived at . . . [and] put them in a safe deposit box or safekeeping of some sort so that if anything had happened to him, they'd have got the summary of his views before he had completed his report."

Norris' concerns were underscored by a registered letter from Frank Hall, vice-president of the Brotherhood of Railway and Steamship Clerks. Hall knew Banks intimately and was worried. His views had changed dramatically from the days when he helped bring Banks to Canada and vouched for him at his citizenship application.

"These are the notes which you requested of me, in connection with Harold Banks of the S.I.U.," Hall wrote Norris. "You stated that they would be considered as confidential; if such was not the case I would have hesitated to put them together, because if they got into the wrong hands it might be that I would be found dead in a ditch some day, with more holes in me than in a colander. However, this is not the time for anybody to have cold feet about a situation of this kind."

The Norris report, which came out in early July 1963, was a devastating indictment of Hal Banks:

> Banks is capable, decisive, egocentric, intolerant and ruthless. He is the stuff of the Capones and the Hoffas of whom dictators throughout history, from the earliest times to the totalitarians, Hitler and Stalin, are prototypes. He is a bully, cruel, dishonest, greedy, powerhungry, contemptuous of the law. In his mouth, the use of the word "democracy" is sheer blasphemy. For him the "big lie" and the failure to remember are ever-ready weapons and shields.
>
> Having read the evidence on this Inquiry, one can readily accept Sheehan's statement that Banks referred to the members of his union as "dumb bastards" for, brainwashing them as he did, he treated them as such . . . . [Banks showed] contempt for his members, contempt for public opinion, [and] a cynical disregard for decency . . . his own personal history of law-breaking, the success of Hoffa and leaders of the I.L.A. in avoiding the compulsion of the law in the United States, and public disinterest brought also contempt for the law. Its processes were to his hand to delay and frustrate his opposition when he could so use them but otherwise the likelihood of conviction was the only condition of his obedience to its rule. . . .
>
> In the S.I.U. of Canada, there was no real democracy, there was the facade and nothing more and the members were so brainwashed and so grateful for the apparent beneficence of which they were recipients at his hands, although the money belonged to all of them, they accepted his dictation without question. Banks' system of conditioning the members to the acceptance of his control is totalitarian. The reaction of the members to that system seems to have been as automatically responsive as the reaction which Pavlov obtained by his methods—a triumph of brainwashing.

Norris noted that without drastic action, Banks' threat could be expected to grow. The report warned that Banks was currying favour with the ILA (International Longshoremen's Association) and the Teamsters in the U.S. in hopes of setting up a new labour federation in Canada. "There is a constantly recurring theme with Banks and indicates his dream of power," Norris warned. "To set up a federation with the Teamsters, the I.L.A., the S.I.U. . . . would, in his words, be 'terrific'. To the average citizen with a knowledge of the activities of Hoffa and the Teamsters and Bradley and Gleason and the I.L.A., and of Banks' activities and the activities of the S.I.U., it might be 'terrifying.' "

The sum total of these problems was, in Norris' opinion, "an emergency situation in interprovincial and international trade." Norris prescribed unprecedented measures: federal legislation putting all maritime transportation unions under government trusteeship. Ottawa would assume the unions' duties, control assets and have powers to investigate financial holdings.

The pressures of the past year were shown in the crisp, aggressive tone of the report and its vigorous recommendations. Those same pressures took a toll on Norris, Wright recalled. "I think he was in his late sixties when he started and I think he was in his middle eighties when it was all over. The fact is that he had a slight stroke within a few weeks after he completed the report and his health just went way down until he died."

20

You're a goddam crook!

Seafarer protester

I agree.

Hal Banks

Hal Banks should have looked like a beaten man after the Norris Commission report was released. Headlines across the country trumpeted Norris' comparison of Banks to Al Capone. News stories documented how he cheated the very soldiers he was supposed to lead. But, through the year that followed, Banks managed to maintain his aura of invincibility, of a man able to pull strings in high places when ordinary measures wouldn't suffice.

The proposed trusteeship didn't just target Banks' SIU: it also cast a wide net over the Canadian Merchant Service Guild, the Canadian Maritime Union, the Canadian Brotherhood of Railway, Transport and General Workers, and the National Association of Marine Engineers. The government wanted the trusteeship to be voluntary. To some union members, this was like being asked to trap a bear, then climb into its cage and tame it.

The CLC's Claude Jodoin preferred to settle the violence on the South Lakes through mediation. Mutual respect and friendship would soothe things, Jodoin hoped. But his personal approach proved to be no match for Paul Hall's influence, and the plan was a miserable failure. Meanwhile, Banks was doing his own lobbying, dropping in on Montreal-area Liberal MPs even before the Norris report was released.

By August, hopes of the CLC ousting Banks and replacing him with the Canadian Maritime Union were all but dead. A young Allan MacEachen, then the new Minister of Labour, announced that the government would push ahead with legislation for a trusteeship to run the five unions in the fall, unless an effective alternative could be found. The CLC, unable to do much else, reluctantly threw its support behind the trusteeship.

By October 1963, Ottawa had admitted defeat in its effort to win a voluntary trusteeship. MacEachen told the Commons that he would be introducing a resolution for trusteeship. Banks' reaction was immediate and unforgettable. He pulled his men off the Lakes and led 2,500 of them to Ottawa. Chants of "King Hal! King Hal!" saluted Banks as he slowly drove up from the Château Laurier, then circled in front of the parliament buildings in his white Cadillac convertible. At his side was a blonde aptly described by United Press reporter Mike Gillen as looking "somewhere between attractive and noticeable."

Thunder Bay MP Douglas Fisher was talking to a couple of Seafarers as Banks circled the Hill, taking his bows for the throng. "This big car crawled past," Fisher recalls, ". . . and I said to one of them. 'Doesn't it bother you, this sonofabitch riding in a Cadillac?' He said, 'Naw, that's the way I want my union boss to be. The best isn't too good.' " It was an attitude that had puzzled Watson and other Norris Commission investigators, who expected that disclosures of Banks' high spending would anger the rank-and-file. "I've never understood it," Fisher said. "It was kind of a feudal thing. But it's certainly there and it's certainly strong."

At noon, Banks dismounted from the Eldorado and marched up the steps of the Hill, chomping on a cigarette and receiving slaps on the back from sailors. "You look good . . . real good," Banks told the strikers and assembled media. "It will be peaceful and it will be orderly. Rest assured of that. These men are not on strike. They are here for justice."

This was too much for one man who happened to be eating lunch on the Parliament Hill lawn. He leapt to his feet and screamed, "You're a goddam crook!" Banks smiled, then waved his Peter Jackson cigarette in the man's general direction and chuckled, "I agree."

Most of the men either cheered or kept their feelings to themselves. The union had a practice of collecting permit books before demonstrations, ensuring strong turnouts. Sailors who didn't attend lost their books and therefore lost their right to work.

The union had placards printed up for the sailors, reading "There are state-operated unions in Russia-Cuba-Yugoslavia-China. Now in Canada"; "The SIU is a democratic union. We intend to preserve it"; "Is this Ottawa or Moscow?"; and "Jodoin sold the SIU seamen down the river." Only a few dissidents dared show up, brandishing signs reading "Go back to the States you bum."

At the height of the demonstration, Banks marched down Parliament Hill alone. A gaggle of reporters took up chase and caught up with him. "What a bunch," joked Banks, who said he was "taking a constitutional." "You're worse than a bunch of sailors." The constitutional brought Banks to a truck from the Montreal Union hall, stocked with ham, cheese and bologna sandwiches for the demonstrators. Banks picked one up, gave it a loud sniff, and then stuffed it into his mouth as the reporters looked on.

Bill Dodge would later say that the only time he really worried about violence from the SIU members was when Banks pulled his men off the job and headed for Ottawa. Dodge's young daughter was friendly with the daughter of George McClellan, commissioner of the RCMP. McClellan learned through his daughter of the Dodges' concerns, and phoned their home in Ottawa. "Don't worry," he told Mrs. Dodge. "We've got a constable on every one of them. We know where they all are. You don't have to worry."

The three trustees were appointed on October 23, 1963. Each had distinguished records: the chairman, Mr. Justice Dryer of Vancouver; Charles Millard, a senior labour statesman; and Judge René Lippé of Montreal. Their immediate problem was to end Banks' strike. Banks told them he'd call a membership meeting that evening in Montreal. He said he'd advise his men to go back to work, but, that he couldn't guarantee they'd follow his advice.

Just a few days after the protest, however, the 100 idled ships were back on the water. Banks proclaimed that the settlement had been reached on his terms. Even those who doubted this couldn't doubt he had won a reprieve. "If anybody tries to dump Banks, we'll strike and back them against the wall again," one SIU executive told 1,500 cheering men as he described a meeting earlier that day with the trustee.

When the next morning's papers quoted Banks' boast that he had struck a bargain with the trustees, then freed the ships to sail again, Lippé bristled. "We didn't promise anything. Why should we promise?" he recalls.

The trustees quickly made clear they did not feel bound to the Norris report, and began a mini-inquiry of their own. "I am willing to believe that anyone is innocent until proved guilty," Dryer told the press. "It's my duty to do that." Recalling the trustees' feelings at the time, Lippé says, "We didn't think we were obligated to put in execution everything that the Norris Commission said. . . . We didn't think our role was strictly to get rid of Banks." Certainly Banks was on his best behaviour: he dropped by the trustees to report to them. It was his charming side, something experienced in the past by victims like Stirling and Greaves before his mood would turn ugly.

As the heat from the Norris Commission dissipated, union figures who had led the fight against Banks reacted bitterly. They were being told to kiss and make up with someone who had raped them. Banks, who had been compared to Stalin, Capone and Hitler, was now being treated as their equal by men who had never suffered his violence. Banks' sudden talk of reform and his cloying civility before the trustees didn't change their opinion of him. On the waterfront SIU threats were still being made towards the CMU. Greaves was still being harassed with calls throughout the day and night. And while the trustees' integrity wasn't seriously questioned, their judgment was savaged. Dick Greaves wrote to MacEachen and the trustees, pleading for change.

Trustee Charles Millard believed there was good in everyone, even Hal Banks. A letter he sent Greaves on February 4, 1964, shows their profound difference in opinion.

While it was good to see you again yesterday in Toronto, I really am very sorry in a personal way that I could not leave you in a happier state of mind.

I know it is easy for someone to say "Don't be so pessimistic," but too often that fails to take into account past experiences and present outlook based on facts as we know them at the time.

Though my outlook is also based on my own experience, I realize and confess that my trade union training was in a very different school and that my heavy reliance on what I consider to be tested policies and principles might not work under the conditions we now face.

I regret too that the CBRT generally, and Elroy [Robson] especially, have taken the critical line they are now pursuing because that will only serve to produce heat where light is needed. All I was trying to tell you yesterday was that if the unions fail to come up with some constructive action, it is now almost certain that it will be taken out of our hands entirely. It isn't good enough to say "it won't work" or "it can't be done" without offering some reasonable alternative.

Suddenly everything changed. On March 18, 1864, Banks was called into the trustees' office and told he was fired. Millard moved into the SIU headquarters, where he could directly supervise the administration of the union. He said he hoped leadership would develop before the next winter's general election.

Dryer brushed off questions on the firing. It was all "too delicate" to be dispensed with at the time, he said. The move came as collective bargaining was about to begin with forty-two shipping companies from coast to coast. "The problem was not with Banks," Lippé recalls. "The problem was with the employers and Banks. It was unworkable so we had to get rid of him. We tried everything we could with the employers to get a rapport with the union going."

The move also came in the wake of revelations that the trustees' phones had been tapped. "I'm not too sure who did it," Lippé says. "I don't think that it was Banks who did it. That has nothing to do with it at all.'' Today, Lippé says he doesn't know who was behind the phone bugging. Then he adds that if he did know, he wouldn't say. At the time, however, Lippé had police protection for his Outremont home for the next week. It passed without incident.

Banks spent that night at home on Lakeshore Drive, snarling ''He's not here'' to pesky reporters who kept calling for comments. He had a daughter, Sylvia, now, from a Croatian immigrant named Marija Guchich. One of Sylvia's earliest memories of life on Lakeshore Road was of the reporters overrunning their lawn as her parents stayed inside, hidden by their remote-controlled curtains.

Reporters, photographers and television cameramen were trooped into Banks' luxury executive suite atop the Seafarers' headquarters on April 21, 1964. The effect, even without Banks, was overpowering. There was still the chrome, green mock leather and electronics of his main office. They were shown his exotic black marble bathroom. They didn't get a look at his kitchenette and bedroom, with their stylish ceramic mural. They were already in the process of being remodelled. The floor that had belonged entirely to Banks was now broken into a conference room and smaller offices.

''There will be changes around here,'' the reporters were assured.

Sure enough, within a few days, workmen arrived at the SIU headquarters to dismantle Banks' enormous, kidney-shaped desk. It took a crew of eight men four hours to dislodge it. The work crew found it was as solid as it was imposing, fastened by bolts to a slab of concrete under the carpet. The workers attacked it with saws, and by the time they left that afternoon, the seat of Banks' power was hacked down to a crescent-shaped hunk of concrete on the floor. Like its creator, it wasn't easily disposed of.

Against token opposition, Red McLaughlin was elected head of the SIU on a reform platform. This horrified many on the waterfront, since the same Red McLaughlin had been Banks' faithful vice-president.

Judge Norris had made it clear in his report what he thought of McLaughlin. "He is devious and adept in carrying out the one-man policies of Banks and in assisting in setting up the farce of democracy in the union," Norris wrote. "He is unscrupulous and it is apparent that much of the abuse contained in the minutes and in reports flows from McLaughlin's pen. . . . Abuses by Banks in connection with the handling of union funds were never checked by McLaughlin. From the evidence, he collaborated with Banks. . . . McLaughlin gave evidence for sixteen days and proved himself to be throughout a clever, resourceful, and entirely untruthful witness on any matters in controversy."

Banks' old enemies couldn't believe what had happened. Banks was still in Montreal and his loyal lieutenant was now running the union.

21

I'm not going anywhere.

Hal Banks, Brooklyn, 1968

There was just the hint of a tear in his eye as Hal Banks stood for the reaching of the verdict. It was May 1, 1964, and finally Banks had been brought to Montreal's Palais de Justice to be tried for the beating of Henry Walsh. The judge in the case was Claude Wagner, whose past verdicts had established him as a tough advocate of law and order. He had little sympathy for Banks. Wagner ruled Captain Walsh's beating was "a manifest act of gangsterism agreed to, prepared, ordered, directed and supervised by the accused" and sentenced Banks to five years in prison for conspiracy to commit assault.

Banks was sent to Montreal's Bordeaux Jail, where prisoners could peek out their windows and see the gallows standing over the courtyard below. Bordeaux was built for punishment, not rehabilitation. It must have been especially confining for Banks, whose spacious penthouse office had now been replaced by a six-and-a-half-by-eleven-foot cell with iron bars on the windows. The big spender was forbidden to carry money; the only book he was allowed to read was the Bible. But his penance would last only two weeks. Chief Justice Lucien Tremblay set his bail at $25,000—only half of what the prosecution had requested. The union paid the bill and Banks was released.

Henry Walsh was mortified. He was still suffering painful reminders of Banks every time he tried to eat a meal or walk, since his teeth had been kicked out in the parking-lot attack and he still limped noticeably. It had taken seven years before Banks was even taken to court, and two weeks after his conviction, he was free again.

Despite the reprieve, however, Banks still faced a large number of other court dates. There was an upcoming trial for the Dick Greaves beating, as well as lawsuits from Walsh, Jack Leitch of Upper Lakes Shipping and former SIU official John Wood. But Banks was nowhere to be found when Wood's wrongful dismissal suit came to court in late August. He had become Canada's invisible man. Word was he had skipped the country for the U.S.

Opposition leader John Diefenbaker boomed and fumed in the Commons about the government's failure to locate Banks. On August 27, Minister of Justice Guy Favreau said he had no information about Banks' flight and reiterated that ''Canadian authorities are presently in touch with United States authorities to obtain whatever information may be supplied to us in that respect.'' Minister of Labour Allan MacEachen admitted that he had heard rumours that Banks had fled to New York, adding he had discussed them with *Toronto Star* reporter Robert Reguly. But MacEachen stressed that they were nothing more than rumours. Insults flew both ways in the House. In vintage Diefenbaker rhetoric, the Opposition leader called Banks a ''pally boy'' of the Liberals. MacEachen shot back that the Tories had chosen to ''anoint and coddle'' Banks when they were in power, since details of the Walsh beating were available in 1957. The charges and countercharges of the October 1 session were particularly rough. Asked once again if he knew the whereabouts of the elusive Banks, Favreau replied limply, ''I am not yet in a position to give the House a precise answer as to the whereabouts of Mr. Hal Banks.'' Then Favreau counterattacked. He noted that the Tories were given RCMP reports on Banks' wrongdoings, including the Walsh beating, on February 23, 1959, and in June 1961. Diefenbaker hit back with an assault that probably did more damage to the English language than the Liberals: ''May I say at once that what the minister has stated is completely untrue as it related to the refusal of the former government to act. What actually happened was that the pampered pet of Liberalism was not proceeded against, and now the honourable gentleman is endeavouring to exculpate himself from his failure to act.'' Diefenbaker then referred to a radio report in which Banks supposedly said he wasn't really hiding and that the government knew where to find him. In full charge, the Conservative chieftain added that it was the Liberal government that had tried Banks on the non-extraditable offence of conspiracy to commit assault, then allowed him to go free.

Unknown to the combatants in the Commons, *Toronto Star* editors Ray Timson and Ralph Allen had just sent Robert Reguly off in search of Banks. For the thirty-three-year-old Reguly, the assignment came as a welcome change of pace. Although he had interviewed Banks in the past, his previous day's story for the paper had been a soft piece on Toronto opera patrons.

Contrary to later rumours, Reguly set off for Brooklyn with no exact knowledge of Banks' whereabouts. ''Nobody tipped me off,'' Reguly says. ''It was just logical. Where else is a guy to go but close to where he's got protection? So that meant New York and San Francisco.''

By the time he got to New York, it was too late in the day to begin the hunt. Reguly strolled Manhattan, taking in the sights of Times Square and the Village. At around ten the next morning the serious searching began with a visit to the office of the National Maritime Union, a bitter longtime rival of the SIU. The NMU staff were more than cooperative, and when Reguly asked for a list of Seafarers' properties around New York, he was given both the list and a NMU muscleman as his chauffeur-protector.

Their first stop was the SIU headquarters, an architectural attempt at grandeur situated in an urban war zone littered with dingy autobody shops and greasy spoons. Someone in the Seafarers' coffeeshop told Reguly that Banks had been by a week ago. There was no trace of Banks at a union training school, so around noon he and his heavy-set companion headed towards the Mill Basin below Flatbush Avenue, where the SIU's yachts were moored. As they drove down Flatbush, Reguly spotted a white Eldorado convertible with distinctive Quebec plates.

''How could I miss?'' Reguly recalls. ''He had to be around.'' And he was.

The fugitive Banks was lolling on a dock by a yacht, a cigarette clenched between his teeth. He looked leaner and more haggard than in his Montreal heyday. His hair had greyed and was combed straight back, a change from his customary flattop brushcut. Reguly made a mental note that he could be wearing a wig.

"Hal Banks?" Reguly asked.

"Ya. Whaddya want?"

"I'm from the *Toronto Star*. I want an interview."

"Fuck off. I don't want to speak to you."

With this pithy exchange, Reguly had the scoop that was to win him his first of three National Newspaper Awards. The young reporter had located Canada's most famous phantom, the man who supposedly had been eluding the combined forces of the RCMP and FBI for more than six weeks. There had been no hot tip, just a logical guess and two hours' work.

An hour later, Reguly was back at the dock with a Kodak Brownie camera he bought, complete with film, for just $15.30 at a neighbourhood variety store. He sneaked up to within fifteen feet of his subject before Banks spotted him and bolted for cover. As he snapped a few photos, four union goons charged him. Something that felt like a blackjack struck his head.

"Somebody said, 'Get him!' " Reguly recalls. "That's all I remember and I just ran like hell." He sprinted up six-lane Flatbush Avenue, his head bloody and the Seafarers on his heels. Reguly's driver pulled a quick U-turn and drew alongside the sailors. Then he jerked the steering wheel and swerved into them, knocking the pursuers into a ditch. "He bounced those guys," Reguly says. "I didn't report that because that's assault or something. He really hit them with the car."

Seafarers in a white Chevrolet joined the chase, but after a few miles Reguly's driver had shaken them off. He pulled up to a donut shop so that Reguly could mop the blood off his head. When Reguly returned to the car, the driver reached under the car seat and pulled out what looked to be a .38 revolver and said, "Don't worry, son, had they caught you, I might have had to use this on them."

Reguly's scoop came at the apex of the *Toronto Star*–Toronto *Telegram* rivalry and spawned a headline that has since inspired a generation of *Star* reporters. The front page of the October 1 night edition screamed, ''STAR MAN FINDS HAL BANKS.'' But even as these night editions rolled off the press, Guy Favreau appeared on the eleven o'clock news with an announcement of his own about Banks. Favreau, his comments taped earlier that afternoon, told the nation once again that he had no information on the whereabouts of Hal Banks. Try as they might, the wily Hal Banks couldn't be found.

The hapless Favreau was pounded the next day in the Commons. He told the House he heard of Reguly's ''alleged interview'' the previous afternoon, but didn't know if it was true. Then, in a bizarre postscript he said that he had ''no way of ascertaining who tipped off the reporter. Whether or not it was Mr. Banks himself I did not know.'' Relishing the wounded Favreau's sorry exhibition, Diefenbaker added a little salt: ''I wonder whether the minister, having tried for so long to find the location of Mr. Banks, is now able to give us information with regard to whether the elusive Mr. Banks, the waltzing Matilda of Canadian politics, has been discovered.''

Diefenbaker's Tories weren't the only ones asking about the sincerity of the Liberal effort to locate Banks. Jimmy Todd expressed the suspicions of many when he charged that ''certain people in the government'' struck a deal with Banks to get him out of the country. ''Diefenbaker was on the right track when he said Banks was only charged with offences on which he couldn't be brought back,'' Todd recalls. ''They didn't want Banks back to tell everything he knows.''

While the Liberals fretted, comedian Dave Broadfoot was onstage in Charlottetown, giving a command performance before Queen Elizabeth. There had been rumours of a possible assassination attempt and the auditorium was packed with RCMP security men. Broadfoot looked at Mounties in the wings, then looked up at Mounties in the rafters. Finally, he snapped the tension by turning to the audience and asking, ''Why are all these Mounties here? Hal Banks has been found. . . . He's in Brooklyn.''

The day after Banks was discovered by Reguly, he was visited by federal marshals. The indignities were immediate, his protests pathetic. ''Do you have to do this to me?'' he asked officers as they arrested him.

He looked softer than he had in his days as a waterfront baron. His pot belly had ballooned and his hair was styled in a curious Julius Caesar cut. Arresting officers didn't get a fight from him. He just muttered that they didn't have to cuff his hands behind his back. Banks shook and ''sighed like a little lamb,'' one marshal recalled, laughing, to *Telegram* reporter Peter Geddes. ''Your big tough guy wasn't even enough for us to get into a sweat over.''

Banks was led into Brooklyn Federal Court for his bail hearing handcuffed between a slender young black prisoner and a slickly attired white man of about thirty, who seemed to enjoy the attention Banks brought. Casually dressed in an open-necked white shirt, Banks kept his head down to avoid the horde of eyes upon him. The pose only accented his fleshy jowls.

Banks was back in the limelight but the fun had worn off, unlike the days of the Norris Commission when he had all but dared authorities to come and get him. Now, finally, they had. And on top of his other problems, Upper Lakes Shipping had jumped in and filed a $5 million suit.

News cameras whirred as he left the court after his first day of extradition proceedings. The fear he had inspired in his Montreal days had evaporated. Crowds stared at him as they might gawk at a caged, drugged bear in a circus. He hid his face, but that only heightened the drama. A passerby wanted to know what kind of prisoner had inspired all that attention. ''Is he a communist?'' she asked. It was but one more indignity to the man once hailed as Canada's great anti-communist crusader.

The next two years were spent in an uneasy limbo, as the Ontario government prepared for their legal assault and Brooklyn-based Banks watched his power within the union dissolve. He kept busy working nine to five at the SIU training school on Flatbush Avenue, protected by a twelve-foot wire chain fence topped by barbed wire.

Banks tried to maintain a low profile, although not to the point of forsaking his white Cadillac convertible. He maintained a dummy apartment in a rundown Brooklyn house. ''Hal Banks'' was on the mailbox but Banks himself was on the penthouse floor of a plush Coney Island highrise, with a view of the Atlantic Ocean and the boardwalk. He had lost much since his days in Montreal, but still at least had a remote-control switch in his Cadillac to automatically open his garage door.

The *Telegram* sent a team of reporters from Toronto to spy on him, and they secretly trailed Banks, Marija and nine-year-old Sylvia. They were touched by the father image he projected:

> He stopped on the way home from work to pick up fruit and vegetables at an open-air market in mid-Brooklyn, [and] collected the family meat from a nearby butcher.
>
> One Sunday he took the brunette he calls Maria [*sic*] and her daughter for a drive through Brooklyn's Prospect Park.
>
> They made a nice trio, Maria [*sic*] in a beautiful silver fox car coat, and white pillbox hat. Her little daughter dressed in a blue dresscoat, with a long pony tail flowing beneath her fluffy wool pixie hat. And Banks suited the upper-class image in his dark coat and hat. But if you looked closely, he was still wearing his favourite red and white flannel shirt underneath and he hadn't shaved well. Sort of hung-over looking.

Years later, Sylvia looked back fondly on the Brooklyn days. She grew up to be pretty like her mother and without any of the less admirable traits one might expect from the offspring of Hal Banks.

Her father placed people in compartments, like tools in a toolbox. Sylvia's role was to give and receive love. She didn't pry into her father's union life or his family history or his days behind bars. She simply loved him as a father and he loved her as a daughter, in an idyllic oasis set apart from the outside world.

"He loves me very much," she recalls, unconsciously still using the present tense for her late father. "It's a kind of love that not too many children go through. God, he used to do everything for me . . . . He used to come home every night with a gift for me."

One December day in Brooklyn, Banks had hidden all Sylvia's Christmas presents on a barge in the Mill Basin, which also doubled as Sylvia's playground. There was a violent storm on Christmas Eve and Marija told Banks to let the weather die down before he went out onto the barge. But Banks ignored her pleas and went out to get the presents so they'd be waiting for Sylvia when she awoke on Christmas morning. ''I used to think Santa really existed,'' Sylvia recalls.

Sylvia remembered one of the first times the nastiness of the waterfront crashed into the loving world she shared with her father. Banks didn't like the way a man crowded Sylvia as he walked with his daughter. Banks slammed a fist into his face and the stranger collapsed. That done, Banks and Sylvia carried on enjoying each other's company. Everything in the world of Hal Banks was back in its rightful place; his enemy defenceless at his feet and his daughter, unquestioning, at his side.

Banks picked at a food stain on his expensive blue suit and enjoyed the show in the Brooklyn Federal Courthouse. His counsel, Abraham Brodsky, held centre stage, flapping his arms dramatically and accusing Canada of playing politics with his client. It was an ironic, confusing and thoroughly entertaining performance. Banks burst out laughing when Brodsky hurled a copy of *Hansard* onto his desk in a grand flourish, only to watch it skid onto the floor.

Brodsky equated Hal Banks with muscular Americanism. If Canada wouldn't extradite Vietnam War draft-dodgers, why should the United States ship back Banks? he asked the court. Clearly, his client was a victim of political persecution. Besides, the U.S.' original extradition treaty was with Britain, not Canada.

''I can assure you that a lot of what has been said here has gone right over my head,'' the commissioner, Salvatore Abruzzo, responded. Abruzzo lacked the power to hold counsel in contempt and it showed in the courtroom behaviour. Quoting from *Macbeth*, Ontario counsel Richard Kuh ridiculed Brodsky's defence, likening it to ''a tale told by an idiot, full of sound and fury, signifying nothing.''

Brodsky didn't need Shakespeare for his reply. ''You say that outside and I'll show you,'' he shouted. Undaunted, Kuh charged that ''rebutting Brodsky is like nailing a custard pie to the wall.''

At one particular low point, Brodsky called Kuh ''devious, sneaky and slimy.''

Pressed for a retraction, Brodsky withdrew the word ''slimy.''

''Act, if not as gentlemen, at least as attorneys,'' Abruzzo pleaded.

Banks' amusement faded when it grew clear the case wouldn't be quickly dismissed. He repeatedly told the guards assigned to him that he didn't understand why the case was continuing. ''I'm not going anywhere,'' he argued. ''What's all this fuss about? I've been living in Brooklyn for years. Everyone knew where I was and now they've got me locked up.''

He was held without bail at the Federal House of Detention, a dingy three-storey red brick building in Manhattan's Lower West Side looking out onto the West Side Highway and truck warehouses. *Telegram* reporter Arthur Cole noted that the constant din of traffic was a marked contrast to the soothing sound of surf he could hear from his seventeenth-floor apartment by the Atlantic. Banks was reportedly a model prisoner, spending much of his time reading.

By Christmas 1967, Banks seemed destined to be returned to his former fiefdom and impending imprisonment. Abruzzo had ruled he should be shipped to Canada to stand trial for perjury. Should that charge fail to stick, Banks wouldn't have to face a term for the Walsh beating. The near murder of Henry Walsh was a separate, non-extraditable offence. Perjury was extraditable while conspiracy to commit assault was not.

Kuh couldn't help but breathe a sigh of relief. He knew that the commissioner's appointment was a political one. It was natural to worry about politics being played at that level. But Banks had lost his case and now extradition should be automatic.

There had been talk that Marija was having visa problems and would be sent back to Canada. But Banks was freed for the afternoon of December 12, 1967, to marry Marija, amid reports that a sympathetic congressman had intervened, putting pressure on the New York Bureau of Prisons to make the happy event possible. It was a simple ceremony, performed, appropriately enough, by a judge. The groom wore one of his dark business suits, the bride, a simple but elegant dress. Marija got a ring and Banks got to shed his handcuffs.

Fewer than a dozen people—including guards—were present, including Banks' best man and longtime friend from the West Coast, George McCartney. When the simple service was completed, the groom and bride kissed. Then the groom boarded a black maria van and was driven back to jail and his dormitory cot. The rest of the wedding party retired to a leisurely lunch.

22

I'm always happy to see justice done.

Banks' lieutenant Leonard ''Red'' McLaughlin rejoices after his boss beats the law

U.S. Secretary of State Dean Rusk sipped sherry with seven lawyers at his inner Washington office on a Friday afternoon in March 1968. He was discreetly entertaining arguments on what to do with bail-jumper Hal Banks.

Banks' former counsel Abraham Brodsky had huffed and puffed and threatened to take the case to the Supreme Court if necessary. But Brodsky had lost and now Banks was represented by the more refined Abraham Chayes and Meyer Feldman. They bypassed the courts and opted for the unusual move of a direct appeal to Rusk.

The tone in Rusk's Washington office was casual, even chummy. Rusk was attentive and courteous as they sat on couches before a cocktail table and discussed what to do with the man who had left Henry Walsh with a permanent limp. ''I had never argued under those circumstances,'' Ontario council Richard Kuh recalls of the meeting's relaxed tone.

If Banks' counsel looked at home, it was because the trip to the State Department was a homecoming for them. Chayes was a former State Department legal advisor and Feldman had served as special counsel to presidents Kennedy and Johnson.

Once the niceties were observed, Rusk's task seemed clear-cut. His own legal counsel, along with U.S. Commissioner Salvatore T. Abruzzo, and the Ontario and Canadian governments were all of one mind: issue an order to ship Banks back to Canada to face perjury charges. History supported them. The last instance anyone could recall of a Secretary of State refusing an extradition request from Canada took place more than a century earlier, when William Lyon Mackenzie had fled to New York in 1837 after the Upper Canada revolt failed.

State Department officials didn't know of another case involving Canada in which a lower court's ruling was overturned on appeal to the Secretary of State. And Banks' lawyers hadn't been particularly convincing. They had tried to argue that the 1842 extradition treaty wasn't binding on the U.S., since it had been signed with the United Kingdom. But Kuh noted that a supplement to the treaty had been signed in 1952, of which one of the signators had been Lester B. Pearson.

When the treaty argument failed, Banks' counsel countered that it wasn't sporting for Canada "to do indirectly what they can't do directly." In other words, Banks was being tried for perjury only because the conspiracy-to-commit-assault charge was non-extraditable. Perhaps it wasn't good form. But no one in power had seemed to mind when the indirect approach was taken by the U.S. to lock up Al Capone, Frank Costello and Alger Hiss.

Rusk, a non-lawyer, shook off more than a century of legal precedent and the advice of his current counsel. In their place, Rusk applied what he called "my old-fashioned sense of justice." He did what Banks' Harvard-educated legal team couldn't do. He found a reason why Banks should stay in the U.S.

". . . Because the charge of perjury in this case arises out of a denial of guilt of a non-extraditable offence, I have concluded it would not be compatible with the overall design or purpose of the extradition treaty . . . to agree to the extradition on the unique facts of this case," Rusk ruled. More than two decades later, Rusk adds: "Furthermore, here was an American citizen who was later in the United States and I felt that any American has the right to affirm his innocence as a constitutional matter."

In other words, if Banks couldn't be extradited for ordering the attack on Walsh, he shouldn't be extradited for lying about it under oath. This reasoning ignored the case of the *United States v. Williams*, where a policeman was convicted for assault and then later found guilty of lying about the assault. The U.S. Supreme Court upheld Williams' conviction, ruling that hitting a witness and lying under oath about it are separate and distinct offences.

But such fine points were irrelevant in the freeing of Hal Banks, Kuh argued. "I'm sure legalities had nothing to do with keeping him in the States," he said in an interview more than twenty years later.

Kuh went into the sherry session having heard that Rusk's legal experts had unequivocally recommended extradition. "One of them [Rusk's lawyers] called me when they got word of Rusk's contrary decision and he was practically in tears he was so personally outraged," Kuh recalls. ". . . Needless to say, I didn't buy a bottle of champagne to celebrate that night. It was outrageous."

Back in Canada, Henry Walsh agreed. The beating had cost him financially as well as physically and he had been preparing a lawsuit against Banks for damages when he skipped bail. Now it seemed like Hal Banks had pulled strings to avoid justice again.

In an odd reversal, some other Canadian labour men in Canada breathed more easily after the decision, while the Liberals pretended to fume. It was a way of locking Banks out of Canada indefinitely. There would have always been the worry he might have been parolled after serving just part of his sentence. Or, even worse, his appeal could have succeeded.

Ontario Attorney General Arthur Wishart would protest that "some pressures were applied" on Washington, as would Upper Lakes Shipping president Jack Leitch. John Diefenbaker would rage that the manoeuvre was purely political.

Meanwhile Red McLaughlin, former Banks underling and now head of the union, would beg to differ. "I'm always happy to see justice done," said McLaughlin, the man Justice Norris had called "devious" and "entirely untruthful . . . in any matters of controversy."

Canada protested and asked for an appeal. Rusk denied the request. Canada asked for an independent international tribunal to hear the case. Rusk denied this as well. Despite the formal denials, Rusk says he wasn't really acting against the wishes of Ottawa. "There was some conversation[s] between members of the Canadian government and members of our own Cabinet, but I would not get into that. . . . We were fully aware of the parliamentary debate on this case in the Canadian Parliament. I'm not going to mention any names, but one member of the

Canadian government said to one of my cabinet colleagues, 'We don't really want him back but there's such a row about this in the Parliament we have to ask for it.' ''

In other words, Ottawa's indignation was a charade. Washington was playing along with them, not opposing them. Who in Ottawa would make such a call? One would imagine that the Ministry of Labour or the Secretary of State's department would have the keenest interest. Repeated attempts to interview then Minister of Labour Allan MacEachen for this book failed while former Secretary of State Paul Martin recalls that he was genuinely surprised by Rusk's move. ''I didn't really know that power existed. I know I did my best to have him brought back to Canada. He should have been extradited according to the treaty of extradition with the United States and Canada. . . . Our courts decided that he should be extradited, but I was not able to get the Secretary of State in the United States to agree.''

Jack Pickersgill, who claims he never once laid eyes on Hal Banks during the union leader's sixteen years in Canada, doubts Rusk's story. Pickersgill says that he is unaware of who might have called Rusk.

Within a couple of months of Rusk's order, Banks was working at the SIU training school, Piney Point, Maryland, which was nicknamed the ''thug ranch'' by one visitor's wife. The thug ranch replaced the Brooklyn training school after a fire in the Mill Basin. It was a place where poor inner-city blacks went with hopes of job training and where Washington politicians went in hopes of a good party. The politicians were seldom disappointed.

The Piney Point camp had a bizarre dual guard system. There were the omnipresent Seafarer thugs and brightly coloured, strutting peacocks. The thugs grunted and swore at strangers while the peacocks screamed horrifically. An impressive flotilla of SIU ships was moored at Piney Point, including the 260-foot *Dauntless*, lushly furnished with a ballroom, saloon, teak panelling and elaborate inset carvings. Built in 1921, it had been auto magnate Horace Dodge's yacht. Now owned by the SIU, as a Washington newspaper reported, it was now for ''almost-nightly parties with union leaders, Congressmen and others.''

Impressed by the SIU fleet, a visitor joked to Banks and Hall, "You've got a big enough navy here to invade Cuba."

Hall turned to Banks, then replied: "Canada first."

It would be the summer of 1968 before Banks and Hall hit the headlines again. Jerry Landauer of *The Wall Street Journal* turned up what was either a major scandal or an unearthly coincidence.

Landauer noted that just days after Rusk's decision was reached, $100,000 appeared in Democratic Party campaign coffers from the SIU's Brooklyn office. It came in twenty packets of $5,000, the legal limit on contributions to committees supporting federal candidates.

The first batch of ten $5,000 cheques was sent on April 3, 1968, almost entirely to committees that had been working for Lyndon Johnson's re-election. This was despite the fact that Johnson announced on March 31 that he wouldn't run. Hall sat tight throughout the tough New Hampshire primary and when his enemy Robert Kennedy entered the race.

Why would the union back Johnson with at least $100,000 when he wasn't running? Landauer suggested that perhaps a deal had been struck when the Banks case was in the balance, and Hall followed through on his side to the letter, even though Johnson had dropped out of the presidential race in the meantime. There is also the possibility that election fundraisers convinced the SIU that the donation would give them influence when in fact it did not.

The $100,000 was the largest single contribution by a union that election year. Despite the SIU's relatively modest size of 80,000 members, the union had reportedly set aside $1 million for political activity in 1968. Republican senator Pal Fannin would argue that at least that much went from the SIU to the Democrats.

The Landauer story made sense to Kuh: "The action of the state department in terms of sound legal action was not explicable. Hence, one had to look at things outside the law."

Bruce Thomas, who acted as one of the SIU lawyers at the

Norris Commission, sees the hand of Paul Hall in the extradition refusal:

> He knew what was going on in the world and he knew how to get things done. Who else could have pulled off the extradition order except a guy in the most powerful position who knew how to pull all of the right levers? . . . I don't think Rusk would have been the guy they would have dealt with. It would have been some fellow on a more political level who would then have probably put it down as labour union guys fighting amongst themselves up in Canada . . . But Rusk, I'm sure, would have been carrying out a request for a political favour for the party . . . I mean, Dean Rusk would have never been close to this crowd at all . . . Canadians have no power at all in Washington . . . It's all U.S. internal politics . . . If you knew how to play the system, as Paul Hall undoubtedly did, he could pull off a major—a major—feat of having a government refuse to turn over a person for a trial in Canada . . . Paul Hall was an immensely effective guy.

U.S. Secretary of Labor Willard Wirtz was pressed by the AFL-CIO to support Banks. Wirtz put in a good word for Banks in a memo to Rusk. While Rusk says he had discussions with Wirtz before reaching his decision, he argued he was not pressured by him. Rusk bristles at the mention of the $100,000 contribution. "That was a completely stupid thing for these union people to do, following that decision of mine that had nothing to do with any pressure or any enticements. For them to make campaign contributions to the Democratic Party was stupid because it was indirectly embarrassing to me and it was just one of those gross things that people do sometimes. I resented it very much . . . I don't know what it was. It was just this maritime union . . . just trying to use its muscle, *ex post facto* . . . It came out of the blue and I deeply resented it."

In the fall of 1968, there were new rumblings that Banks still might be extradited. The Republicans had been elected and Republican senator Paul Fannin was pushing hard to have Banks shipped north. Since Banks had been saved by executive and not judicial action, he could be extradited by executive action.

John Turner, then the new minister of justice, told the House on November 20, 1968, that he had contacted Crown legal advisors to see if Ottawa could reclaim Banks. "It is the view of the United States counsel, supported by the view of law officers of the Crown, that the extradition proceedings are at an end, and that the incoming United States administration cannot reverse the decision taken by Mr. Rusk and order Mr. Banks re-arrested and retained for extradition to Canada."

But seven months later, while pressures to extradite Banks had cooled, an avenue to bring him north remained open, according to a confidential White House memo. Legal advisor George H. Aldrich wrote Secretary of State William Rogers that: "Our Embassy in Ottawa advises that the Canadian Federal Government does not have any great interest in reopening the case, and reports from our Canadian posts generally indicate that the Canadian political interest stems more from attempts to embarrass the Canadian Federal Government than from an interest in the return of Mr. Banks . . . . As a matter of law, the Canadian Government is free to make a second request through the courts for the extradition of Harold Banks."

Toronto *Telegram* reporter Bob MacDonald uncovered the memo in the third week of November, 1969. Earlier in the fall, Turner told the Commons that the matter could not be reopened before the courts and was exhausted. George Hees, PC for Northumberland, said he was shocked by the memo. "It shows clearly that the U.S. had been told our Federal Government was just going through the motions—that it really didn't want Hal Banks back . . . . The truth is that the Government fears Banks will tell all about his activities if he has to come back—he'll spill all about his dealing with the Liberal Government here . . . . He is just is just too dangerous for our Federal Government to want him returned."

Philip Carlip, the SIU's Washington lobbyist at the time, said he doubts that there was any real pressure from Ottawa to extradite Banks. "If they [Canada] had wanted him, they'd have gotten him."

To say that Banks tested Paul Hall's patience is to say Stalin and Hitler had a falling out in the Second World War. Banks had been a major embarrassment for the union throughout the Norris Commission, as well as a huge financial drain. Paul Hall's ambitions in the AFL-CIO certainly weren't helped by the Banks' debacle. In an unguarded moment, Hall had said, ''The commission started out to get one man and wound up punishing a whole union. It would have been a better situation if someone had taken Banks out and shot him and then the union would have been left alone.''

Hall had tucked Banks away at the Piney Point base, but Banks refused to fade away. He wanted the top Piney Point job, held by Robert Matthews, a thirty-year administrator with the SIU. When Banks began campaigning for the job, Hall demanded that he lay off. ''You don't know what you're doing,'' Banks replied. Hall exploded and Banks was instantly unemployed. Banks packed Marija and Sylvia into the Caddy and set out on a holiday that lasted more than half a year.

''He wanted me to see [the] United States all over,'' Marija recalls. ''We were through twenty-eight states. We took [a] trip for seven months. We travelled by car and we stayed in hotels and motels . . . . He was just like a little boy and happy.'' Sylvia slept in the back seat of the Eldorado as they toured the U.S. Banks wasn't working but money wasn't a problem. While he relaxed on the road, nerves were also soothed in Ottawa and Piney Point. ''We're not one bit sorry he's gone,'' a SIU Piney Point official said. ''The guy was always trouble for us.''

23

His life wasn't that easy, believe me.

SIU vice-president Ed Turner describes the final years of Hal Banks

By the 1970s, it was getting harder and harder to reconcile the myth of Banks with the reality. The myth was that of the black knight of the labour movement, who fought more, gave more, took more, spent more and screwed more than anyone else dreamed imaginable. He was the communist-fighter–turned–rogue who turned a foreign country into his own personal fiefdom, where he lived above the law.

The reality of Banks in the 1970s was that of a fat man growing fatter, a weak man growing weaker. Even his enemies wished he had died in a blaze of glory instead of decaying before their eyes. He was a man of the 1930s and 1940s who reminded people of ugly, violent times they'd just as soon forget. Banks the myth was at least entertaining. Banks the reality was an embarrassment.

He was also expensive.

Bay-area shipping unions contributed at least $50,000 to a war chest to help out Paul Hall after his costly defence of Banks before the Norris Commission. And when Banks returned to California, he was given a stipend of $450 a week, coming in equal portion from the Sailors' Union of the Pacific, the Marine Firemen, and the Marine Cooks and Stewards' Union. Word was that strings were also pulled to get Banks a prime marine spot to dock his forty-foot yacht, the *Malabar*. It was in a pleasant spot about two miles from Fisherman's Wharf and directly facing Alcatraz Island.

Banks hadn't lost his bluster, but he had lost the goons and government connections that backed him in Canada. Sometimes he'd pull out a book of phone numbers from his Montreal days and brag about what powerful people he used to be able to call. But the names meant little to those living in the San Francisco Bay area, and often Banks preferred to boast about the large house he used to own in Pointe Claire.

While Banks terrified people in Montreal, in San Francisco he just annoyed them. And when sailors around the Bay area got into their cups, they'd sometimes joke that they should kidnap Banks, drag him back across the border into Canada and hand him over to the Mounties. While no attempts were made, the prospect of a return to Canada was no laughing matter. He wouldn't risk getting on a plane because he worried they might be diverted north by fog or overfly their destination and end up in Canada, where Banks still faced a five-year prison term for the Walsh beating. "If they'd take me up to goddamn Canada, they'd hang me," he'd say to his friend Vic Rahauge.

Banks couldn't forgive Paul Hall for firing him, and he plotted against the SIU leader. He formed an unlikely bond with SIU official Morris Weisberger, who was bypassed for Hall as SIU leader. The glue of their relationship was said to be their common disaffection for Paul Hall. And when Hall died in 1979, Weisberger stopped returning Banks' calls. The relationship dissolved, leaving Banks no one with whom to conspire.

Some Canadian union men believed Banks headed south with incriminating documents, tapes and photos of highly placed union, government and business figures. On the west coast waterfront, no one particularly cared about the compromised Canadians. But word was that Banks also brought with him material that was damaging to Hall as well.

SIU official Ed Turner resented the sniping at Hall. He decided to stop paying Banks his $150 a week and the marine cooks and stewards and firemen followed suit. "I figured we were paying for a debt we didn't owe," Turner said. So with his allowance dried up, Banks stepped up his campaign for a pension.

Banks used the *Malabar* to run the harbour pilots out to ships. He'd regale them with stories of how he'd soon be rich from running supplies to supertankers. He figured he could cash in on the oil crisis by racing alongside the oceanliners and shuttling supplies to them as they sailed.

Banks had lost his power, but not his nerve. He offered a job on the *Malabar* to Gunnar Hexum, the man who hired him into the SUP three decades before. Hexum, who considered hiring Banks one of the worst mistakes of his career, declined the offer.

Banks had respect as a sailor, if not as a man. He seemed to always have a different awestruck young sailor working on the *Malabar*, cleaning the engine or making repairs. When it came time to pay him, Banks would shout, "Aw, get the hell out of here." If asked about the firing, Banks would answer, "Well, the guy looked like he was gonna steal something."

For an old union man, Banks wasn't ticklish about violating picket lines. "He was pretty rough," Stitz said. "I remember when I went out to get on a ship there and a picket boat tried to get in between us. The guys on the picket boat hollered something about being a scab . . . . Anyhow, I got on and took the ship wherever they were going . . . Hal went back and got his car and drove over and picked me up. He had a couple of clubs put onboard. I was going to stay there to do some more ships. He alerted me that . . . 'Those FB's are going to come back here and try to get us. Here's your club. I'm going to go home and I don't know whether to bring my gun down or not.' I said, 'Forget it, I don't want to be part of a battle.' Shoot, he was right at home with things like that. He loved that."

Harbour pilot Don Hughes is a big, strapping man who wasn't afraid of Banks or many other men. His wife had died when his son was five and he was praying that someday he'd meet the right woman. Marija Banks knew the feeling.

One day Hughes approached Banks to say that Marija was leaving Banks for him.

"You?" Banks said. "I'm gonna shoot her with a shotgun."

"Hey, listen. If you're gonna shoot at her, you're gonna have to shoot at me. What's wrong with you anyway? Shape up. These things happen."

"You should know about her," Banks warned. "I'm gonna tell you. Well, never mind. I'll let you find out for yourself."

During Banks' heyday in Montreal, it would have been unthinkable for anyone to take his wife or one of his girlfriends. He was the one who took other sailors' wives. But the old Banks was apparently dead. And while Banks let go of Marija, he clung to his money. Marija got the "Castro" lamps and the rest of the furniture, their china and appliances and just $2,500. Banks was awarded the two launches—the *Malabar* and the *Sylvia*—as well as his 1968 Cadillac and whatever fortune he had squirreled away. Since it wasn't in a bank account, Marija couldn't touch it.

Banks also dodged paying court costs, filing that he was a poor seventy-year-old indigent with a net monthly income of just $366.40. For Hughes and Marija, their meeting was a godsend. They married in 1978 and had a son two years later.

The *Sylvia* was Banks' second boat and carried his hopes of making it big again. It was just a shell, but he had dreams of equipping it. He wangled free harbour space for it from the harbour pilots. But one day the *Sylvia* broke loose from her moorings and scraped against some other boats. Banks took the harbour pilots to municipal court to sue for damages, despite the fact that they had been giving him free pier space.

When Banks entered the courtroom for the suit, he stopped dead. Surely he had seen a ghost: a familiar angular face leaned towards him as he sat in the witness box and asked, "Mr. Banks, have you ever been convicted of a felony?" Banks almost jumped out of the witness box. His interrogator was John Droeger, the man Banks was rumoured to have had murdered in 1955 in Baltimore.

"*You* were convicted of a felony," Banks screamed, losing his temper completely. "You were! You were!"

Word on the Montreal waterfront was that Banks had Droeger killed in 1955 in the United States, after paying hundreds of thousands of dollars to bring an ocean liner into Philadelphia. The story was only half true. Banks paid the money to bring the *Challenger* into Philadelphia, where Droeger was picked up by the FBI on draft-dodging charges. After spending a year and a half in jail, Droeger was pardoned by Lyndon Johnson and drifted into a career in marine law. One of his strangest and most memorable days behind bars came on a sports celebrity day. Mixed in with visiting athletes was one of Banks' henchmen. Droeger took the visit as a lightly veiled threat from Banks.

Droeger took the harbour pilots' case for old times sake. "I just did it for fun—to see if I could get a rise out of him," Droeger laughs. "It was kind of goofy. It was just a silly thing. The bar pilots were pissed off at him because they had given him the use of the pier."

Everyone except Banks involved in the suit took a break for lunch together, then strolled down to the *Sylvia* to survey the damage. Banks refused to accompany them, still furious over Droeger's questioning. The judge looked at the small dent on the boat and snickered. He asked why they didn't just drop the suit and fill in the hole with polyfiller.

Banks was awarded $1,000, a fair sum for the dent but only a fraction of the damages he sought.

One of Banks' adversaries during the *Sylvia*'s legal troubles was walking alone on a wharf one day carrying a bucket of water. He heard a popping sound, then a laugh. He looked up and saw Banks racing off in a boat, cackling. Then the Banks' foe looked down and saw that someone had shot a hole in his bucket.

The *Sylvia* never did make it to the ocean. Even after Banks' death, the city was still threatening to sue for the damages it caused when it had crashed into other boats. The last Banks' SUP friends heard of the *Sylvia*, it was run aground on a mud bank.

Sylvia was a good daughter, helping Banks aboard the *Malabar*, cooking meals and keeping him company until she fell in love and married. There were rumblings that Banks didn't approve of his son-in-law's Jordanian nationality. Medical problems were his major worry, however, as his heart and stomach deteriorated.

Banks was now in his early seventies, living alone on the *Malabar* at the marina, where dock fees were less than rent for a small apartment. Banks appeared broke. He pestered the shipping unions to help out with his $250-a-month payments for dock space. It was the least they could do, since they hadn't given him a pension, Banks reasoned. However, life on the *Malabar* was cheap, if not particularly comfortable. The boat was outfitted with a sonar system Banks had fashioned himself with parts taken from two other systems. With it, he was able to locate salmon around Alcatraz, making fishing easy, if unsporting. And because it was homemade and comprehensible only to Banks, there was little danger of anyone stealing it.

Apparently reduced to social security, Banks no longer seemed to care how he looked. Old associates were startled to see him tramping about in shorts, looking more like a bum than the man who once had owned hundreds of custom-made suits.

Back in the 1950s, reports had trickled out of Montreal that Banks was stashing money away in the U.S. Some of the rumours came from no less a source than his ex-wife Helen. By the 1980s people wondered what had happened to Banks' money, since it was assumed that if Hal Banks had money, he'd show off with it. When he stopped showing off, it meant he was out of money. But others were sure he had money cached in locations known only to Banks. He was faced with huge medical bills. If he declared his wealth, he'd have to pay taxes on it and pay his own medical bills. If he appeared poor, he could get a free ride.

24

He never really forgot. He lived in the past a lot.

Friend Johnny Wilson describes Banks' memories of Montreal

When he was working on the *Malabar*, Banks seemed to be happy enough. But as his health declined, so did the condition of the boat. Soon, both were unseaworthy.

Banks' heart had deteriorated to the point that when he visited the Sailors' Union hall, people would have to come down to the entrance to meet him because he couldn't climb the building's stairways. While he had once used gadgets to spy upon others, he now relied upon one to control his breathing. He often wheeled a little cart with a breathing apparatus that held tubes inserted into his nose. In addition, his stomach-muscle problems gave him the appearance of a bloated, beached whale.

A SUP secretary was stunned by how much he had changed. He had once been dapper, maybe even handsome. "I had to look twice," she said. "I thought, Jesus Christ, that's Hal Banks. I guess his sins caught up with him. He could barely waddle. God, he was ugly. To me, he was a gruesome sight."

Banks had smoked three to four packs of cigarettes a day well into his seventies. Marija would warn him he should quit smoking, watch his eating and ease up on his work. But Banks ignored her. "He would—you know—get very upset if I was to give him advice," Marija recalled.

Banks' health collapsed when he took a tumble from the *Malabar* onto the dock and then into the water in the mid-1970s. At first he tried to ignore the ache in his shin. But two days later, it had swollen so badly that he couldn't pull on his pants. When

Banks went to a hospital, the doctor immediately began prepping for an operation.

"No, I don't want an operation," Banks said.

"Actually, right now it's a matter of where to cut your leg," Banks was told as the doctor pointed to the two points where he might amputate the limb. "Either from here or from here." However, Banks was adamant that nothing would be done to his leg. So the doctor prescribed some medication and sent him home. Eventually, the swelling subsided but Banks was never the same.

Next came the stomach-muscle problem, which Banks blamed on a surgeon. He told his buddy Vic Rahauge that in the middle of an abdominal operation, his surgeon had turned to an intern and said, "Goddamnit, I have to catch a plane. I'm going to be late. Here you take over." Banks then explained that the intern forgot to sew up all his stomach muscles, which meant he now had to wear a stomach supporter.

"Oh bull, Hal!" Rahauge said. "No doctor's gonna leave you right in the middle of an operation."

"Bullshit," Banks said, then repeated his charge, adding, "if he wasn't such a good friend, I'd have sued the sonofabitch."

"Well, he wasn't a very good friend. Why don't you sue him? Christ, didn't they knock you out when they were doing all that stuff to you?"

"Sure they did, but I could hear what they were talking about."

Banks told his son-in-law Fayyad that he had almost a million dollars until his health fell apart. "He said that he spent almost all of his money on doctors," Fayyad said.

Banks would bring Fayyad with him on trips to the doctor to act as a witness. Fayyad would be positioned beside the doctor and whenever the physician said something, Banks would turn to Fayyad and ask, in a deep and totally serious voice, "You hear that?"

Doctors wanted to operate on Banks to open up his veins and improve circulation, but he refused.

"Jesus, Hal, you ought to do it," his friend Johnny Wilson warned.

''The death rate in that stuff is way high. Better than ten per cent,'' Banks replied.

Wilson asked doctors about the procedure and its death rate. ''They said that if it was even close to one percent, we'd never use it,'' Wilson said. He tried again to talk him into it, but had no luck. Banks needed to be in control, not drugged on an operating table totally at the mercy of others. Death meant a loss of control, but as long as he was alive, he was in charge.

At the age of seventy-five, Banks decided to head fifty miles north to visit the Wilsons in Napa, California. The visit would last from July 4, 1984, until February 27, 1985.

''We thought, well, the poor devil had no place to go,'' said Johnny Wilson, a harbour pilot. ''He actually had no place to go.''

Tracey Wilson said Banks was able to relax inland and away from the waterfront.

''I think the water kept him a little excited,'' she said. ''He'd think about the old days and want to get back on the water.''

And when he missed that excitement, Tracey Wilson would remind him of their full-sized swimming pool.

''Oh, go on out there and sit by it and just pretend,'' she'd say. Banks never swam, but he often went poolside and let his mind wander.

''He'd sit out there and look in it, watch the shadows in it.''

Other times, he'd sit alone with his ukelele, playing ''My Dog Has Fleas'' and other tunes that would entertain ships' crews decades before.

''He could sure play that thing when he wanted to,'' Tracey said. ''I came in one morning and he was playing. I said, I thought you said you didn't know how to play that. He said, 'Oh, I can play a few things. . . .' ''

He told Tracey Wilson that his name was in the *Encyclopaedia Britannica,* which is true. ''Harold Chamberlain Banks'' appears in the 1964 edition, sandwiched between ''Banking'' and Kurdish nationalist ''Mustafa al-Barzani.'' It was the only thing he had to be proud of, Banks said, not mentioning that the brief reference compared him to Adolf Hitler, Joseph Stalin, Jimmy Hoffa and Al Capone.

Banks told the Wilsons that as a young boy in Iowa, he worked in a bakery to help his parents make ends meet. He'd bring them home leftovers or things not good enough to offer to the public. In the following years, he said, he was a spirited teenager, and was constantly getting caught by his father in compromising positions with girlfriends.

The Wilsons and everyone else close to Banks could see he adored Sylvia. He spoke of her constantly and fondly, and would phone her in San Francisco two or three times a week. Tracey Wilson was sure he preferred having a daughter to a son: "He was partial to little girls. His daughter Sylvia was the apple of his eye."

"Anything that Sylvia wanted, Sylvia got that was within his means," Johnny Wilson said.

He'd brag of how she could swim like a fish when she was just a tot and chuckle at how high her rear end would stick into the air as she splashed about.

He told of a trick he played on Sylvia back in Piney Point. She was in about grade four then and was supposed to grow a watermelon as a class project. Banks had one of his helpers from the union till their garden, then they planted the seeds.

One hot afternoon Banks decided to speed things up. He and his helper went to a supermarket and bought a watermelon. They set it in the garden, then arranged weeds around it like watermelon leaves.

Sylvia was thrilled but puzzled. She asked why the watermelon was so cold on such a hot day.

Banks stayed quiet.

One of Sylvia's favourite memories of Piney Point was the day her pet rabbit went missing. She ran into her father's seamanship class, crying. Banks stopped the class and lifted her onto his lap.

"Oh, daddy, my rabbit is gone," she cried.

Banks told her that the rabbit's parents had come by to take it home.

''Well, Sylvia,'' he said. ''You know how it is. The rabbit misses his mommy and daddy.''

As a house guest, Banks was alternately fun, pitiful and obnoxious, as the Wilsons found out. For someone who had invited himself and who didn't pay board, he had no compunctions about trying to run the Wilson household. He wanted control over everything, from Tracey's hairstyle to how Johnny built a new porch. When he took over the cooking, Tracey didn't mind since she thought he was better in the kitchen. But he also let her know he wasn't impressed with how she washed clothes. ''He told me I didn't know how to wash,'' Tracey Wilson recalls. ''I didn't use the kind of soap he did. I use Wisk and he used All. And he said he would do his washing because I would burn his up. He always took the time to look at all the ingredients it had in it. . . .

''He sort of took over. But then, he was always used to being boss. I think that was what he was doing.'' Like lawyer John Schlesinger years before, Johnny Wilson sensed the way to ward off Banks was to stand up to him. ''I used to have to set on him. I threatened to throw him out a couple of times. Then he'd start crying to the wife. . . . The minute somebody jumped right back at him, he'd clam up. Then he'd go right back to normal. He wouldn't be the big *I Am* that he thought he was. . . . If you stood up to him, he'd back off completely.''

It was hard to stay angry at a man in Banks' pitiful condition. Sometimes, in the wee hours of the morning, he'd get short of breath and start to panic. He'd bang an old shovel handle on the ceiling of his basement room until the Wilsons came down to help. After an hour or so of conversation, he'd sometimes relax, then say, ''I feel better now. I'm relaxed. I'll go back to sleep.'' Other times, the Wilsons would drive him to a hospital. After a couple hours of observation, he'd be pronounced relatively fit and released.

Banks' union friends in San Francisco assumed he had run

out of money, but Johnny Wilson knew differently. Banks was in the habit of leaving money with him before going into the hospital. On one trip he left $47,000 in cash with Wilson, who put the money into the bank. When Banks came back for it, the bank told him he couldn't have the whole sum in cash, so Wilson took cashiers' cheques. Banks exploded, saying they were too difficult to cash.

After that, Wilson would hide money for Banks.

"When he was up here at the house, he had $90,000 dollars in cash. I know that personally. I saw it. He kept it in a paper bag."

The paper bag was hidden in a lamp, Wilson said.

"Hal used to pack between $1,800 and $2,000 in any denomination of bills in his pocket at all times," Wilson said. "He always had cash in his pocket. Plenty of it." Despite the wad of money, however, Banks waited attentively for his social security cheques to arrive and let the state pay his medical bills. And every three months, he mailed down a cheque to pay for his dock space. Johnny Wilson's sure his bills were up to date at the marina until the end of February 1985.

It was then that he decided to head back to San Francisco, to Sylvia; his infant grandson Walid, and son-in-law Fayyad.

People would later say that Banks died broke but Wilson says this simply isn't true. "I know when he left this house here on the 27th of February [1985] he had pretty close to $90,000 in cash. He had a stack of bills there that was three or four inches thick."

Before leaving, Banks and Johnny Wilson had a bizarre argument.

"He gave me a letter that the boat and everything went to me," Wilson recalled. I said, 'Listen Hal, I don't want no part of the money or the boat. If you leave this goddamn thing in my name, anything happens to you, the boat and everything goes to Sylvia.' "

"Well, I don't want her to have it," Banks replied.

"Too bad," Wilson said. ". . . I had this letter where everything was signed over to me. . . . The day he walked out, I said, 'Here's the letter, Hal. It says I own the *Malabar*. You have the money. Now tear this letter up right in front of me.' And he tore it up right in front of me and threw it in the garbage can."

Banks didn't thank the Wilsons for his seven months of free board, but they didn't expect him to. ''Hal figured the world owed him a living,'' Johnny Wilson said. ''He wasn't a bad man to have around. He got a little obnoxious at times. But you had to set on him a little bit, and then he was all right.''

''He never did say so, but I think he was grateful,'' Tracey Wilson adds. ''He made me awfully angry at times, but I got over it. He was a nice guy. I miss him.''

25

I couldn't decide if I was hypocritical or forgiving.

Former Seafarer Eddie Mackin describes his emotions at Hal Banks' funeral

On the day that Hal Banks bought a set of tires for the Cadillac Fayyad sensed something different about his father-in-law. There had been a time when Banks never drove an Eldorado more than a year old and only with the best Michelin tires on it. Now Banks had settled for a used set of tires with 20,000 miles on them. ''Hal, those are cheap tires,'' Fayyad said, surprised that Banks was no longer buying top-of-the-line goods.

''Oh, what the hell, I don't think I have long to live,'' Banks replied.

Banks was alternately accepting and denying the fact that death was near when he moved in with Sylvia, Fayyad and Walid in the spring of 1985. ''He was the type of man that . . . would think he would never die,'' Sylvia says. ''He would never talk about death . . . I think as you get older, you get scared. You don't want to face the fact that some day you're going to leave.''

Old habits from the waterfront didn't leave Banks when his power did. When he met new people, he'd probe for ways of controlling them. ''He digs and digs and digs and digs until he finds something about you, and then that is the lever,'' Fayyad states. For Fayyad, a native of Jordan, the lever was his visa. Banks told him that as a U.S. citizen he had the right to check up on him.

When Banks sensed a power struggle with his son-in-law, he'd offer dark warnings such as ''Well, I don't think you'll look very good if I go to immigration and tell them about you.'' Fayyad learned to deal with these remarks, however. ''When something like that happened, I just ignored him.''

Banks held out hope for Fayyad, who juggled driving a cab with studying civil engineering at university. He told him that his life was sweetened by a packet of sugar. It was an unverifiable story that Banks enjoyed repeating. Banks told of how awful coffee was in jails and how prisoners were denied sugar. When Banks was heading out to strike duty that promised to get violent and possibly lead to jail, he'd pack sugar packets. The sugar also helped buy friends, something essential for a prisoner.

One day he gave his sugar to a top union official.

''Oh, thank you very much,'' the leader said. ''Look me up when you leave.''

''After that, everything got started,'' Banks told Fayyad.

Democracy remained alien to Banks. When he, Sylvia and Fayyad would watch television, Banks always wanted to be the one to pick the show. He loved to match wits with Judge Wapner of the daytime show ''People's Court.'' As he watched he'd make side comments to Fayyad on the law, including his theory on why it's smart not to have a bank account. ''When you don't have a bank account, you're judgement-proof,'' he'd tell Fayyad. Other favoured TV fare were current-affair political shows and old John Wayne movies.

Sometimes Sylvia and Fayyad would want a say in what programs were selected. ''Let's compromise,'' they'd protest.

''Okay, what would you like to watch?'' Banks would ask, then turn the channel to whatever show was mentioned. Then, a minute or so later, he'd switch the channel back to Judge Wapner, John Wayne or whatever else he wanted to watch. Often while he did this, he'd be sharpening knives until the blades were perfect.

Other times, Banks would work on his model boats. Sylvia and Fayyad lived next to Golden Gate Park, where ducks and seagulls share manmade Spreckels Lake with a model-boat club. The club has special plugs that are handed out to members using

Spreckels Lake to control the frequencies of the remote-operated boats and, it is hoped, prevent crashes. Banks would have no part of it. His six-foot sailboat was twice the size of most boats on the lake and he outfitted it with a UHF plug, which removed it from any controls other than his own. He loved to race it right up to the edge of the cement pool. Then, just as it was about to wreck on the shore, he'd crank hard and veer it back to open water, delighted by the ''whish'' it made. Hal Banks had gone from violating the laws of international waterways to flouting the guidelines of the Spreckels Lake model-boat club.

After four months at Sylvia's home, Banks moved on to the home of Magda King, an old girlfriend. While based there, he was frequently trying to sell the *Malabar*. The boat was badly run down now. Where it was once a marvel of maintenance and gadgetry, it was now unsafe to take to sea.

He wanted the Sailors' Union to buy it from him and allow him use of it without any financial responsibilities. SUP president Paul Dempster says that by the end of the summer of 1985, Banks owed more than a thousand dollars for marina rental space, and feared that the *Malabar* would be offered for public auction.

Dempster said he put in a call to Ed Turner, SIU vice-president, who in turn called his union's president, Frank Drozak. Dempster also called around to other unions, explaining the *Malabar* could be used for picket duties. The SIU got back to Dempster, saying they didn't want any part of anything to do with Hal Banks. No reason was given, and the other unions quietly backed away from the proposal. That left only the Sailors' Union, and Dempster said it couldn't afford to take on the boat on its own.

If the unions wouldn't buy his boat, they could at least pay for his dock rental, Banks reasoned. It didn't seem like too much, considering he wasn't even getting a pension. Dempster said at one point Banks concocted a scheme which had him giving the *Malabar* to the SUP. This too was turned down. Gifts from Hal Banks were considered more trouble than they were worth.

''He came here one day to talk to Morris [Weisberger] and I,'' Dempster recalls. ''He couldn't come up here because there's no elevator and he couldn't go up the stairs. He couldn't breathe. He carried a machine with him so that he could breathe.'' It was a pitiful sight, but many within the SUP felt no need to bail out Banks. "We make our own beds," an officeworker said, "and his life wasn't exemplary."

Dempster finally relented and bought the *Malabar* for $4,000, the price of an outboard engine. When some SUP members grumbled that they shouldn't be giving Banks handouts, Dempster argued that the *Malabar* could be used for training young seamen at the union's Harry Lundeberg School of Seamanship. Banks' cheque came through while he was in the hospital. He wanted cash, but was in no position to bargain. Word would sift back to Paul Dempster that some unsavoury characters were hanging around the hospital, waiting for him to be paid.

Tom Zee of the SUP dropped by the hospital to see Banks. Zee brought Banks a union belt buckle and windbreaker, signifying the SUP's one-hundredth anniversary. Zee was shocked by how much weight Banks had lost over the past year through his illness. Banks' new windbreaker hung loosely on his once imposing frame. The weight loss made his huge hands seem all the more disproportionate. Zee had always thought they'd be more in place on a grizzly bear than a human.

"Sit down, sit down," Banks urged. "Have a talk. Let's talk." Then Banks showed that he hadn't lost all his spark.

"Go get me a jug," he told Zee. Zee declined getting him alcohol, and just chatted.

After a week in hospital, Banks was moved out of intensive care. Fayyad told Sylvia now was the time to ask him about money. It might look bad, but the option was that the money could be lost forever. And they needed it. Sylvia was pregnant again and she and Walid had run up expensive medical bills over the past year. They needed the money and Fayyad assumed that Banks would want Sylvia and her family provided for.

Fayyad and Sylvia knew Banks had money but they didn't know how much he had or where he had stashed it. Banks had once mentioned that he had hidden gold bars in the engine room of the *Malabar*, then moved them. Fayyad had found numerous combinations to locks written on scribbles in Banks' papers but had no clue as to what they would open. Only Banks knew how much money he had and where it was hidden. And as long as he was convinced he wasn't going to die, he wouldn't tell anyone—including Sylvia—about his finances.

Banks had tubes running into his nose and couldn't talk. Some people had been in to visit him before Sylvia and Fayyad did. Banks had scratched out notes for them. When they asked about the stashed money, Banks kept raising his hands as if to say, "Don't worry." Two days later, Sylvia came back and tried again. "How much does Magda have?" she asked, referring to his girlfriend.

Banks kept telling Sylvia not to worry. He felt he was getting better; regaining control. There was no need to disclose what he had or where he had hidden it. "Don't worry," he soothed. Then he added an enigmatic comment Sylvia and Fayyad couldn't explain, "You'll be taken care of, even if you have to go to court."

A couple of days later, Paul Dempster got a desperate call from Sylvia. She was crying. Her father was brain dead and being kept alive by a machine. Should she tell the doctors to pull the plug on her father and let him die? Dempster told her that if he were in Banks' position, he'd want the machine shut off. But he added that it was her decision.

A few more days passed before Sylvia called him again. Her father was dead. How could she pay for the funeral? The cremation was six hundred dollars and she was broke. "How are we going to bury my poor papa?" she wanted to know.

Dempster spoke to other unionists and they decided they'd pay for the service, if nothing else could be arranged. "He died penniless," Turner says, reflecting standard wisdom on the waterfront.

"Everybody helped Banks at the end. Not much, mind you. Just a couple hundred dollars. When I'd visit him on the boat, I'd try to give him a little."

Of course, things weren't nearly so simple. Johnny Wilson was adamant that Banks had $90,000 in cash when he left Napa, and that his dock rental was paid up to that point. He may also have stashed money with other people. Considering Banks' paranoia about trusting others, it's doubtful that he had left all his money with Wilson. And when Banks last spoke to Sylvia, he had told her where to look on the *Malabar* to find her inheritance. But when she got there, there was no money to be found.

Banks' lawyer Geoffrey Rotwein states flatly that Banks never left money with him and that Banks never even let on he had money. Banks' girlfriend Magda King also couldn't help Sylvia out. But eyebrows shot upwards when a previously poor waterfront crony of Banks' bought a top-of-the line Mercedes Benz just after Banks died. Johnny Wilson also has suspicions about the young men Banks used to dupe into helping on the *Sylvia*. One of them left in a huff that summer, charging Banks owed him money and refusing to return some of Banks' tools. Word was he had a key to the *Malabar* as well.

There are also the shady characters Dempster heard about hanging around the hospital, waiting for Banks to be paid for the *Malabar*. And there's the less sinister possibility that Banks simply forgot where he left the money. He was, after all, seventy-six. As his health declined, he was prone to lapses of memory. Whatever the case, Johnny Wilson feels sorry for Sylvia. ''She got a raw deal,'' he says. ''A damn raw deal, I think.''

Tom Zee would spend a week cleaning out the *Malabar*. Dempster had told him to go through the boat with a fine-tooth comb in case Banks had stashed his lost fortune there. Instead, Zee found old mattresses and junk. When he unloaded the junk, the *Malabar* rose six inches in the water. Zee also found a baffling labyrinth of wiring. All the wires were the same colour, making them comprehensible only to Banks. While Banks had the reputation of being a master electrician, there was an ominous burn mark near one clump of wiring. ''It was a miracle he didn't have a fire,'' Zee said.

Zee also found a radio scanner, which had allowed Banks to listen in on passing ships and the police. It was doubtful anyone else could get any use from it, since Banks had fashioned it himself. Another discovery was an enormous collection of keys strung together by a wire. There was no clue as to what they would unlock.

Nowhere did Zee find any money.

Paul Dempster spoke to other unionists who knew Banks and they decided they'd pay for the funeral out of their own pockets if nothing else could be arranged.

And so Banks received his final rites across the street from the SUP hall at the Apostolate of the Sea church. His friends weren't quite sure which church he had been born into, but it didn't really matter. Hal Banks' only god was himself and he told his friend Johnny Wilson that he didn't believe in an afterlife.

No one from Canada made the trip down for the funeral. Fewer than a dozen people showed up, and that small group was not overcome by grief. Only Sylvia cried.

October 11, 1985, was what Captain S.W. Robeson of the ocean-liner MV *President Eisenhower* called "a fit day for the man of the sea to be buried." The *Eisenhower* was en route to Yokohama, Japan, when it stopped at 44 degrees 35 minutes North longitude; 176 degrees, 38 minutes West, at four in the afternoon. The weather was overcast, with a light rain and a westward wind.

As the ship stopped, Robeson addressed his crew:

> We are gathered here today to commit the last remains of a brother seaman Harold C. Banks. Harold Banks was born on February 2 [*sic*], 1909. He sailed on several ships as AB [able bodied seaman] and Bosun. As a union brother Harold Banks was sent to Canada by Harry Lundeberg Sr. to organize ships for the SIU. He succeeded and remained to become the SIU president in Canada as well as becoming an international vice-president for North America for the SIU. On September 24, 1985, Harold died.
>
> I never personally had the pleasure of sailing with Harold Banks. I didn't know what he believed in, but I hope and pray that whatever God he believed in has welcomed him with love and mercy.

As Banks' ashes were committed to the sea, the captain continued:

> Harold C. Banks, unto God's gracious mercy and protection we commit you. The Lord bless and keep you. The Lord make his face to shine upon you, and be gracious unto you. The Lord lift up his countenance upon you, and give you peace, both now and evermore.

> Unto Almighty God we commend the soul of our brother departed, and we commit his ashes to the deep; in the sure and certain hope of the resurrection unto eternal life, through our Lord Jesus Christ in whose coming in glorious majesty to judge the world, the sea shall give up her dead. Amen.

That said, the *Eisenhower* sounded a farewell salute and moved slowly ahead through the falling rain. It was an anonymous end for an infamous man.

EPILOGUE

Hal Banks' presence still hangs heavily and oppressively over the Seafarers' International Union of Canada, more than two decades after he fled Canada. The leader of the union today is former Banks bodyguard, Roman "Shotgun" Gralewicz. He refused to talk to me about his years with Banks, other than to remark, "It was excellent. What else can I say?"

The SIU is indeed excellent for Gralewicz, if not for the average sailor. It remains the dominant sailors' union on the Great Lakes, although its numbers have slipped to just over 5,000 members. Gralewicz has been its top official since 1973, when he took over from Leonard "Red" McLaughlin. McLaughlin slipped quietly from the union's presidency to a post as the Seafarers' Ottawa lobbyist. (Coincidentally, Liberal warhorse Jack Pickersgill worked out of the same Ottawa office block as McLaughlin, writing a memoir of his glory days at the hub of power.) McLaughlin moved on in the early 1970s to a post in Geneva with the International Labor Organization. While there had been a storm of protest when Banks represented Canada before the ILO in 1954, few noticed when McLaughlin joined the organization's staff, on the recommendation of the Ministry of Labour and Canadian Labour Congress officials.

Gralewicz and McLaughlin aren't the only former Banks' lieutenants to have landed on their feet after his departure. One ex-official is currently a sergeant on the Montreal police force. Former west-coast boss Norm Cunningham has moved to the other side of the bargaining table, as chief negotiator for the B.C. Maritime Employers' Association. Former official Don Swait went on to become a Teamsters officer in Toronto.

In 1974, ten years after Banks found sanctuary back in the U.S., Justice Norris was calling for another federal commission into the union's activities after charges of violence, blacklisting, intimidation, rigged union elections and sweetheart contracts. Reformers complained that Gralewicz, whom Norris characterized as "one of Banks' goons," was abusing the hiring hall system, essentially giving him ultimate control over who works. They also grumbled that the union had shipped $100,000 of their dues back to the SIU office in Brooklyn. There were still charges that the union was indecently close to the federal Liberals. For his part, Norris suspected that the union was still being run by Paul Hall from the U.S.

Gralewicz will tell anyone within range of his booming voice that times have changed. ''The stigma of Banks is still here,'' Gralewicz said in 1976. ''Today's unionism is a different ball game; it's a different era. Banks is past—just like the old robber barons of industry. Banks had his era. Then there was the McLaughlin era. Now it's the Gralewicz era.'' But the image of Papa Hal has served Gralewicz well and Shotgun Roman isn't about to put Banks' ghost to rest. Young sailors at the union's training institute in Morrisburg, Ontario, still are taught to sing, ''Hal Banks, he started it all, all the way from Montreal. . . .''

Dissident Seafarer Don Davis might well have thought that the spirit of Banks was still around after campaigning against Gralewicz in the union's 1983 election. Davis was worked over by Mike ''The Boxer'' McManus in the union's Toronto hall as friends who tried to rescue him were held off by SIU officials. Davis ''deserved everything he got,'' a Seafarers official told members. The union then hired high-profile lawyer Eddie Greenspan to defend McManus and Peter White, a Thorold, Ontario, patrolman also charged with the beating. McManus and White were jailed, none the less, for what the Crown called a ''contract assault.'' When White was freed, Gralewicz elevated him to the position of Toronto port agent, working in the same hall where Davis was pummelled.

When *Globe and Mail* reporter Lorne Slotnick asked him about Davis, Gralewicz retorted, ''A fathead like him, I don't need anybody to help me beat him up. I'm 56 years old and I can slap him silly. But he's just a big fat ass, I'm telling you, and I mean that sincerely.''

The Canadian Labour Congress, which readmitted the SIU in 1968, did nothing more than squirm uncomfortably when union reformers urged a probe of the Davis case. When the CLC was first faced with the Seafarers' problem in the late 1950s, the congress was in its infancy and lacked constitutional remedies for gangsterism. Today, union members still are in need of workable protections for free speech, fair elections and appeals against bogus trials. They are, according to labour economist John Crispo, "still vulnerable to whatever kinds of ruthlessness leaders want to impose."

It's to Canadian labour's shame that the SIU was kicked out of the Canadian Labour Congress for raiding members from other unions, not for gangsterism. The unspoken message was that stealing members was a worse offence than cracking skulls. And almost thirty years after the original problem arose, the CLC still lacks an internal code to deal with unethical practices, although it does have an ethics code for international unions.

Banks thrived in Canada in a legal and ethical vacuum. One can't escape the feeling that much more could have been built on the efforts and courage of men like Harry Crowe and Henry Walsh. It's not enough for labour to wring its hands, shrug its shoulders and commiserate with victims of labour injustice. For a body so quick to call for the regulation of other parts of society, labour has adopted an oddly laissez-faire attitude concerning its own abuses.

"Over the past 40 years, . . . unions have been transformed from voluntary secret associations of workers into bureaucratized quasi-public agencies," *Toronto Star* labour reporter John Deverell argues. "They are certified and granted exclusive bargaining rights by the state. In Ontario, all employees in certified bargaining units are now required by law to pay union dues. Clearly the state has a right and an obligation to enforce minimum standards of democratic conduct and accountability within unions in return for the legal privileges and protections they enjoy."

Conditions aboard ships did improve during Banks' reign in Canada. Whether they improved because of Banks is a moot point. Ship's captains were no longer allowed to buy the cheapest food possible, then pocket what was left of their food budgets. Safety was also given more attention. Sailors in Montreal had the benefits of the union's luxurious St. James Street headquarters, with its medical clinic, library and pool tables.

Although Banks didn't negotiate any pension plan for his members, he did bring in a vacation plan. But fewer than a quarter of the members actually received any vacation benefits. Gerald Swartz wrote in his graduate thesis for the University of Illinois that wages went up more than 100 percent during Banks' rule, although ''it is difficult to determine whether the increase in Canadian maritime wages was due more to the union's bargaining strength or to the pace-setting increases which occurred in the United States.'' In either case, it should be noted that wage increases only applied to those sailors who stayed in Banks' good graces. They were no help to the estimated 10,000 sailors put on the Do Not Ship list without trial.

Banks left an indelible stain not only on the Canadian, but on the U.S. maritime labour movement. His career marked a watershed, as cynical manipulation gained an upper hand over idealistic radicalism.

''When you really come right down to it, the Canada incident was where the SIU and the SUP lost their political halo or their political virginity,'' Sailors' Union of the Pacific historian Stephen Schwartz remarks. ''Before that, you had a lot of people in the SUP and SIU who were anti-communist but considered themselves anti-communist radicals. . . . The sailors' union for a long time did not recover from the sense of disappointment and the sense of a break—a rupture—with tradition.''

The rupture took place in two distinct stages. The first was the SIU's replacement of the Canadian Seamen's Union in 1949–50. ''There was a lot of dissension and anger and embarrassment over that,'' Schwartz said. ''Deeply felt. But in the later years, in the period of the late 1950s and early 1960s, it was just felt that Banks was a horrible personal embarrassment to the SUP and the SIU.''

Schwartz got a phone call from the RCMP at his San Francisco office in June 1986. It was nine months after Banks had died. The Mountie, who said he wanted to clear up the fugitive's files, asked for confirmation of Banks' death. Twenty-one years after Hal Banks fled Canada, the RCMP had finally got their man.

INTERVIEWS

The following people were interviewed for this book and whenever possible, interviews are taped. Other sources who did not wish to be identified include former Seafarers' International Union staff executive members and acquaintances of Hal Banks.

Fayyad Almasri, son-in-law of Hal Banks, interviewed September 21, 1986

Sylvia Almasri, daughter of Hal Banks, interviewed September 21, 1986

Knud Andersen, member of Sailors' Union of the Pacific since 1940s, interviewed June 4, 1986

James Anderson, former police chief of St. Catharines, interviewed November 16, 1985

Dave Beck, former head of United Brotherhood of Teamsters, interviewed June 27, 1986

Jacques Bellemare, lawyer, interviewed September 1, 1986

Guy Bernier, ex-Canadian Seamen's Union and Seafarers' International Union Canadian District patrolman, interviewed August 7, 1986

Jim Bryan, former St. Catharines policeman, interviewed November 16, 1986

Mrs. Ivan Buchanan, widow of former St. Catharines Mayor Ivan Buchanan, interviewed November 15, 1986

Philip Carlip, retired Seafarers' International Union Washington lobbyist, interviewed September 15, 1986

H.K. Carson, former CBRT organizer, interviewed May 6, 1986

Donald Crichton, former neighbour of Hal Banks, interviewed August 6, 1986

John Crispo, economist, interviewed November 25, 1986

Jean Crowe, widow of CBRT research director Harry Crowe, interviewed January 14, 1986

Dan Daniels, former editor of the Canadian Seamen's Union newspaper *The Searchlight*, interviewed September 12, 1986

Harry Davis, former president of Canadian Seamen's Union, interviewed September 9, 12, 1986

Paul Dempster, President, Sailors' Union of the Pacific, interviewed June 4, 1986

Bud Doucette, former officer of Canadian Seamen's Union, interviewed September 9, 1986

Howard Draper, former RCMP officer, interviewed May 9, 1986

Frank Drea, former Toronto *Telegram* labour reporter, former international representative of United Steelworkers of America, former provincial Conservative cabinet minister, interviewed January 10, 1986

John Droeger, lawyer, former sailor, August 20, 1986, interviewed September 12, 16, 19–21, 30, October 22, 1986

Senator Joyce Fairbairn, former United Press International reporter, interviewed September 3, 1986

Ellen Fairclough, former MP for Hamilton, interviewed May 4, 1986

Douglas Fisher, journalist and former NDP Port Arthur MP, interviewed March 20, May 28, 1986

Jack Geller, lawyer, interviewed November 19, 1986, February 13, 1987

Bill Gilbey, longtime Communist Party of Canada member, interviewed May 9, 1986

Michael Gillen, former United Press International reporter, interviewed May 27, 1986

Joe Grabek, former Canadian Seamen's Union patrolman, interviewed September 13, 1986

Colin Gravenor Sr., former public relations man for Hal Banks, interviewed May 23, 1986

Richard Greaves, former National Association of Marine Engineers president, interviewed November 15, 17, 1985, February 27, March 16, April 21, 1986

Percy Guralnick, bailiff, interviewed June 28, 1986

Peter Gzowski, journalist-author, interviewed April 14, 1986

William Hamilton, former Montreal city councillor and MP, interviewed September 13, 1986

Walter Harris, former Immigration and Citizenship Minister, interviewed March 21, May 2, 1986

Captain Michael Harrity, ship's captain, interviewed September 19, 1986

Dr. Eileen Herridge, daughter of former NDP MP Herbert Herridge, interviewed August 19, 1986

Gunnar Hexum, former Sailors' Union of the Pacific organizer, interviewed June 13, September 19, 1986

Françoise Houtman, widow of Canadian Seamen's Union official and Upper Lakes Steamships Personnel Manager T.J. Houtman, interviewed September 13, 1986

Marija Hughes, former wife of Hal Banks, interviewed September 20, 1986

Tony Jiunta, tailor, owner of Tony the Tailor shop, interviewed July 21, 1986

Syd Katz, journalist, interviewed April 16, 1986

Kaj E. Kristensen, business agent, Sailors' Union of the Pacific, interviewed June 4, 1986

Richard Kuh, counsel for Ontario at Banks' 1967–68 New York City extradition hearing, interviewed August 20, 1986

Marc Lalonde, junior counsel to Industrial Commission as to Shipping in the Great Lakes and St. Lawrence River System, Former Finance Minister of Canada, interviewed January 23, May 12, 1986

Pat Lavelle, former assistant to Labour Minister Allan MacEachen, interviewed June 26, 1986

Pierre Lefebvre, psychologist, Bordeaux Jail, interviewed July 19, 1986

John Leitch, head of Upper Lakes Shipping, interviewed November 11, 1985, October 8, 1986

Leon Levinson, former Montreal reporter, interviewed January 25, 1986

René Lippé, former trustee for federal trusteeship of Canadian Maritime Unions, interviewed January 24, 1986

Wilf List, former *Globe and Mail* labour reporter, interviewed April 17, 1986

Gunnar Lundeberg, official, Sailors' Union of the Pacific, interviewed June 4, 1986

Peter Maas, author *The Valachi Papers, Serpico, The Rescuer, King of the Gypsies, Marie, Manhunt* and *Made in America*, interviewed September 3, 16, 1986

Edward Mackin, former foreign representative, Seafarers' International Union, interviewed June 3, 1986

Paul Joseph Martin, MP 1935–68; Secretary of External Affairs, 1963–68; interviewed May 18, 1986

Jean McGough, widow of John McGough, former National Association of Marine Engineers executive, interviewed May 7, 1986

Tom McGrath, former officer of Canadian Seamen's Union, national vice-president of CBRT, interviewed September 6, 1986

Mrs. John McNamara, widow of John McNamara, Welland Canal lockmaster and CBRT Local 212 president, November 11, 1985

William I. Miller, lawyer, interviewed September 9, 1986

Harry Mockeridge, former president of Montreal Steel and Foundry Workers' Union, interviewed August 7, 1986

Lawrence Morrissey, U.S. prosecutor, interviewed August 20, 1986

Peter C. Newman, author-editor, interviewed April 17, 1986

Sergeant Steve Olynyk, former RCMP anti-subversive squad member, interviewed, January 24, 1986

Art Paquette, former official of Montreal Steel and Foundry Workers' Union, interviewed August 7, 1986

Jack Pickersgill, Department of External Affairs, 1937; served in various capacities in Prime Minister's Office, 1937–1952; Clerk of the Privy Council and Secretary to the Cabinet, June 1952–June 1953; Secretary of State, June 1953; Minister of Citizenship and Immigration, 1954–57; Secretary of State, 1963–64; Minister of Transport, 1964–67, interviewed April 11, September 30, 1986

Vic Rahauge, former San Francisco pilot, interviewed August 22, 1986

Robert Reguly, former *Toronto Star* reporter, interviewed January 14, 19, 1986

Henry Rhodes, former Canadian Labour Congress organizer, interviewed May 4, 15, 1986

Robert Rice, former Canadian Press reporter, interviewed June 27, 1986

Philip Ross, labour historian and writer, interviewed September 5, 1986

Geoffrey Rotwein, lawyer, interviewed August 20, 1986

Eddie Roworth, former *Toronto Star* reporter-photographer, interviewed April 16, 1986

Claude Roy, controller for Koumy Investments Inc., owners of former Seafarers' International Union hall at 634 St. James St., interviewed August 6, 1986

Dean Rusk, former U.S. Secretary of State, interviewed August 26, 1986

John Schlesinger, lawyer, interviewed August 7, 1986

Stephen Schwartz, labour historian and author, interviewed May 12, June 2, 3, 4, 5, 6, 1986

D.N. Secord, former CBRT executive, interviewed May 6, October 9, 1986

Clayton "Red" Sinclair, former Montreal *Gazette* reporter, interviewed January 13, 1986

Michael Starr, former Labour Minister, interviewed May 1, 1986

Perry Stitz, bar pilot, interviewed August 22, 1986

John Stirling, former National Association of Marine Engineers and Canadian Maritime Union officials, interviewed May 6, 1986

Peter Stursberg, author, interviewed March 19, 1986

Bruce Thomas, lawyer, interviewed July 7, 1986

Ivan Timonim, former CBRT researcher, interviewed May 3, 1986

Mrs. Agnes Todd, widow of Jimmy Todd, SIU reformer and Canadian Maritime Union founder, interviewed November 11, 1985

Ed Turner, executive vice-president, SIU-AGLIWD, vice-president, SIU International Union of North America, AFL-CIO, interviewed June 5, 1986

Alma and Hugh Wallace, former Pointe Claire residents, interviewed August 8, 1986

Captain David Walsh, instructor at Nova Scotia Navigation School, member of Company of Master Mariners of Canada, interviewed September 18, 19, October 1, 1986

Captain Henry Walsh, former officer of Canadian Merchant Service Guild, interviewed August 29, October 1, 1986

Phyllis Walsh, wife of Captain Henry Walsh, interviewed October 1, 1986

Alan Watson, accountant, interviewed January 9, October 25, 1986

Edwin Wilson, former Seafarers' international representative and Central Intelligence Agency agent, interviewed July 4, 1986

John Wilson, bar harbour pilot, interviewed August 20, 1986

Tracey Wilson, wife of John Wilson, interviewed August 20, 1986

Stan Wingfield, former Canadian Seamen's Union member, interviewed September 7, 1986

Maurice Wright, lawyer, interviewed November 28, 1986

Thomas F. Zee, instructor, Andrew Furuseth School of Seamanship, Sailors' Union of the Pacific, interviewed June 4, 1986

Current owners of Banks' Pointe Claire home, names withheld by request, interviewed July 17, 19, 1986

INDEX

GLOSSARY OF ACRONYMS

AFO—American Federation of Labor
CIO—Confederation of Industrial Organizations
CSL—Canadian Steamship Lines
CBRT—Canadian Brotherhood of Rail and Transport Workers
CLC—Canadian Labour Congress
CLSU—Canadian Lake Seamen's Union
CMU—Canadian Maritime Union
CSU—Canadian Seamen's Union
ILO—International Labor Organization
ITF—International Transport Workers' Federation
LSU—Lake Sailors' Union
NAME—National Association of Marine Engineers
NMU—National Maritime Union
NSU—National Seamen's Union
SUP—Sailors' Union of the Pacific
SIU—Seafarers' International Union
TLC—Trades and Labor Congress